PUBLISHED BY AMERICAN HERITAGE
PUBLISHING CO., INC.
NEW YORK

BOOK TRADE DISTRIBUTION BY MEREDITH PRESS

INSTITUTIONAL DISTRIBUTION BY HARPER & ROW

D-DAY

THE INVASION OF EUROPE

BY THE EDITORS OF AMERICAN HERITAGE

The Magazine of History

NARRATIVE BY AL HINE

CONSULTANT S. L. A. MARSHALL

Brigadier General, USAR, Ret.
Chief Historian,
European Theater of Operations

Foreword

We have here a story not simply of a great victory in war but of one of the outstanding human achievements of all time. Operation Overlord was the Allied design to invade France and liberate Western Europe from Nazi tyranny. How it was begun — on D-Day, the sixth of June, 1944 — will be understood as these pages unfold.

Because there is military glory enough in what happened on that day to warm the American heart through several generations, I prefer to think of it as a superb human effort that dared and achieved the impossible. The task was infinitely larger than any that men had tried in former times, and we may be sure that we will never see its like again, such are the limits set on bold adventure in the atomic era.

Measured in purely mathematical terms, the liberation of Western Europe was a monumental deed. Yet the giant build-up of war goods needed to smash Hitler's forces was the smaller aspect of the task. A stricken land had to be healed and an oppressed people provided with new foundations for productive lives. Their transportation system had to be restored, their factories rebuilt, their ports made whole. These things were done, and because of it, world freedom still has a future.

In these days, when cataclysmic forces, concisely packaged, may be delivered by a few hands to wipe out the treasure that mankind has created through the centuries, it is not easy to make seem impressive the figures which marked a new Everest in mortal endeavor. To dig and keep free the Panama Canal over many years required the movement of 72,306,000 tons of earth, steam shovels picking it up here and laying it down there. To stage the D-Day invasion and to maintain the European Theater of Operations for one year required an equal tonnage of war matériel, most of it transported across oceans and narrow seas, amid peril.

You will read in this book about the Mulberries. Work was begun on them on June 7, and twelve days later a great hurricane hit and smashed these monstrous man-made harbors. When Mulberry A drowned, the number of small ships sunk with it and the tonnage of cargo carried to the bottom equaled the disaster to the Spanish Armada in 1588. Still, across the beach, unloading proceeded under conditions which, by past military theory, would have made it impossible to maintain a major campaign.

Thus, the courage to dare the impossible, the same courage required to parachute into the very lap of the enemy or to wade ashore into a deadly cross fire. It also took a special brand of bravery for men to land in France on D-Day armed with only a camera or a sketch pad. The photographs they took and the paintings they made from their on-the-spot sketches are a vital part of this story.

What was wrought in Europe is not only for the archives so long as the possibility — nay, the certainty — remains that in times to come Americans must revive the essential spirit that energized the achievement this book honors.

S. L. A. MARSHALL

General Eisenhower visits American paratroopers sc
uled to drop behind the German lines early on D-

Six new AMERICAN HERITAGE JUNIOR LIBRARY *books are published each year. Titles currently available:*

Contents

COVER: *Heavy German shellfire rakes the American assault forces at Omaha Beach on D-Day.*

COMBAT ART SECTION, U.S. NAVY

FRONT ENDSHEET: *Among the first to land, engineers tackle the beach obstacles at Omaha.*

ROBERT CAPA-MAGNUM; COURTESY *Life*

BACK ENDSHEET: *British armor lumbers ashore; one tank (right) blazes after a direct hit.*

IMPERIAL WAR MUSEUM

1.

Setting the Stage

A brisk breeze left over from the English winter blew carelessly through an open window of the British War Office in London in May of 1944. With the impudence of winds everywhere, it whisked twelve copies of closely-typed orders from a desk, blowing them pell-mell into the crowd of pedestrians on the pavements below. Workers in the office, from top staff officers to secretaries, raced down to the street after them, for these free-flying sheets were Top Secret — the instructions for the coming invasion of German-occupied France by thousands upon thousands of Allied assault troops. They contained the most vital and secret information of World War II.

Eleven copies of the missing document were recovered easily, but the twelfth could not be found. To lose one was as bad as to lose all, for this information in German hands could wreck the whole Allied offensive. Two

agonizing hours passed. Finally, a British sentry, standing duty on the opposite side of the street, turned in the missing copy, which had been handed to him by a stranger; to this day no one knows the identity of the passer-by who held in his hand the fate of the Allied armies. The officers breathed a great sigh of relief and went back to work.

The decision to invade Nazi-held Europe across the English Channel had been made two years before, in April, 1942, when German, Italian, and Japanese forces were on the march. At that time, there was a chance of Axis victory over the scattered and disorganized Allied nations.

In the next two years, however, before the cross-Channel invasion became a reality, the tide began to turn. The Russian Army held, and Adolf Hitler's mulish fury destroyed valuable Nazi divisions in the overextended front. The Royal Air Force beat back German air attacks on England itself, and new waves of RAF and American Army Air Force bombers carried the air war deep into Germany.

There had been thoughts of a European invasion for 1943, but the decision to put full muscle into the invasion of North Africa did not leave enough Allied strength for a strike into France as well. The North African landing of American troops and the continuing grim vigor of the British desert fighters destroyed the German and Italian armies there. By the end of 1943, British and American troops had driven deep into southern Italy. In the Pacific, United States forces had rallied and were island-hopping relentlessly toward the Japanese homeland.

Another vital factor was tipping the scales of war in the Allies' favor: the conversion of American industry to a war footing. Guns, ammunition, tanks, planes, ships, uniforms, rations— the hard core of war without which no army can operate— poured out of American factories in numbers never before even imagined and were sped to the war fronts around the globe.

The United States even shipped and set up whole factories overseas. In Iran, for instance, there was an airplane assembly line, with hooded Arabs and Iranians putting together fighter planes, which were in aerial combat over Stalingrad less than twenty-four hours after Russian officers accepted delivery at the plant. The American mass-production economy that Hitler had scoffed at was proving to be one of his most dangerous enemies.

Even though the tide was turning against the Axis, the cross-Channel attack had to be made, and it had to be made successfully. The German war machine must be hit and crippled on the Continent. Unless Hitler's army was forced to fight its enemies in the west as well as in the east, the war could drag on indefinitely.

The Allies faced a grim problem. Failure of an invasion attempt at this stage of the war would deal a crushing blow to morale throughout the free world. It would mean an immense loss of life among the assault forces and the destruction of weapons and equipment that would take years to replace. In the wake of an unsuccessful cross-Channel punch, Germany planned to transfer as many as fifty divisions from France to the Russian front. England would lie vulnerable to the onslaught of a new arsenal of secret weapons which the Germans were preparing to launch from French bases— V-1 jet-propelled "buzz bombs" and giant V-2 rockets. The invasion was a necessary and dangerous gamble.

Invasion planning began immediately after the go-ahead in 1942. General Dwight D. Eisenhower landed in England that June to head the United States Army in the European Theater. Direction of the North African landing was still ahead of him, and he did not assume supreme command of the European invasion until January, 1944. At the time of his arrival in 1942, United States forces in the British Isles amounted to only two incompletely trained Army divisions and a handful of Air Force detachments.

The bulk of the combined British

Securely housed in thick concrete casemates, big coastal guns, one of which is seen here in a German photograph, were a major threat to any cross-Channel invasion. These batteries were in the chain of fortifications Hitler called the Atlantic Wall.

and American invasion planning was complicated and routine—the endless collection of more and more troops and equipment in England, and the endless conferences of top-ranking officers of both armies with each other and with the proud and touchy Free French movement of General Charles de Gaulle. There were decisions to be made co-ordinating the invasion plans with other war efforts around the world, and the never-ending evaluation of reports on everything from German strength across the Channel to long-range weather forecasts. Over and above all this were the RAF and the USAAF, bombing German key points, photographing enemy installations and supply lines, and keeping a constant watch on the distribution of Nazi power along the French coast.

These phases of invasion planning were conventional; there were others that deserve to be called fantastic. Tried out, but never put into operation, was a scheme for freezing sawdust and ice together to form a floating platform that could be used as a temporary dock and even as a landing strip for small planes.

No less fantastic, but quite workable, were the huge floating steel-and-concrete artificial harbors called Mulberries, to be towed into place after the landings. With such harbors, supplies and fresh troops could be brought ashore until ports were captured from the Germans.

There were also the Gooseberries—artificial breakwaters made up of rusty old ships, to be sunk offshore to insure sheltered water for the landings—and Pluto, the code name for under-Channel pipelines through which fuel for tanks and trucks could be pumped directly from England without danger of German air or submarine attacks.

All these, and many other unusual and specialized inventions—such as amphibious tanks, tanks to cut paths through fields of land mines, and aluminum foil to be scattered from planes to deceive enemy radar—were included in the invasion planning.

When General Eisenhower took active command at the beginning of 1944, one of his first acts was to enlarge both the striking force and the target area. Later events were to prove the wisdom of his decision.

By this time there could be little doubt in anyone's mind, Allied or Axis, that an invasion was going to take place. German submarines sank three million tons of Allied shipping in 1943, but this was a small loss compared to the shipments that arrived safely.

Merchant ships, military transports, and luxury liners carrying thousands of soldiers zigzagged past mines and U-boats, unloaded at British ports, steamed back to America, and returned swollen with new loads. England became a giant arsenal. It was a favorite joke that the island would sink under the weight of men and equipment were it not for the counter-pull of hundreds of huge antiaircraft balloons that floated overhead.

There was not even much doubt about the general date of the invasion. It was almost certain to be in spring or early summer of 1944. Weather made any earlier date unlikely.

Field Marshal Erwin Rommel, the brilliant German commander of the North African desert war, now serving on the French coast, noted constant invasion alerts in his diary throughout March and April and May. German military intelligence officers reported that Allied troops across the Channel were in a "high degree of readiness."

There was also little uncertainty about where the invasion would strike. Any invasion force from England al-

These men played leading roles in the D-Day assault. Seated left to right are Sir Arthur Tedder, Deputy Supreme Commander; Dwight D. Eisenhower, Supreme Commander; and Sir Bernard Montgomery, who was to lead the ground forces. Standing left to right are Omar Bradley, U. S. 1st Army commander; Sir Bertram Ramsay, naval commander; Sir Trafford Leigh-Mallory, chief of the air forces; and Walter Bedell Smith, General Eisenhower's chief of staff.

most had to strike between Brest and Calais— an impressively long stretch of coast, but by no means impossible to defend. The Pas-de-Calais region closest to the British shore seemed the most likely. For that reason it was the most heavily guarded, but the Germans were not so stupid as to neglect building a so-called Atlantic Wall along the entire length of the Channel front.

Field Marshal Gerd von Rundstedt, Rommel's immediate superior and commander-in-chief of the German armies in conquered France, had his own theory of invasion defense. He would hold his heavy striking power well behind the coast line until the landing was made; then, taking advantage of the confusion of the invaders and their supply problems, he would counterattack with every man, gun, and plane he had. Rommel, on the other hand, felt that the first twenty-four hours of the invasion would be crucial, and that defenses should be arranged to knock the invader back into the sea before he could win even a toehold on the beaches.

This disagreement ended in a compromise. Von Rundstedt's master plan still held, but Rommel, since taking over the coastal command in November of 1943, had set up ingenious de-

Two of the thirty-one concrete breakwater sections of a Mulberry— a huge artificial harbor— near completion in an English shipyard in April of 1944. Some were built of rubble from England's bombed cities.

16

German Field Marshal Erwin Rommel, his Iron Cross medal around his neck and his tank commander's goggles pushed up on his cap, was photographed with his staff during training exercises in Normandy, prior to D-Day. Next to him, wearing glasses, is his chief of staff, Major General Hans Speidel. Put in charge of the Atlantic Wall defenses, Rommel had won fame earlier as the wily "Desert Fox" of the North African campaign.

fenses on almost every foot of beach that might tempt an invader.

Sharp prongs of iron and steel with explosives mines attached lurked under the waves to demolish landing craft. Scores of heavy artillery batteries, securely planted in concrete casemates, lined the French shore. Pillboxes stood back of and on the flanks of most beaches, mounting machine-gun nests able to rake the area with bullets. Millions of land mines were cunningly hidden along the coast. In some cases, Rommel installed elaborate flame throwers capable of scorching key beach areas with belching fire. He was tireless in patrolling the coast line, improving defenses as his sharp eyes caught any weaknesses, devising new ways to add to the impregnability of Hitler's *Festung Europa*— Fortress Europe.

Since there could be no secret about the approximate time and place of the invasion, the only secrets remaining— secrets that had to be kept at any cost — were the *exact* time and the *exact* place of the assault. Here the Allies successfully bluffed the enemy.

The beaches of Normandy had been chosen as the assault area, but counting on German suspicion of the Pas-de-Calais as the target, the Allies established an elaborate hoax to keep enemy attention focused on that sector. General George Patton, as well-known to the Germans as any other Allied commander, was cast in the role of "Pas-de-Calais invasion leader."

A headquarters was set up for him at Dover, directly facing the Pas-de-Calais. It was surrounded by hordes of dummy tanks and aircraft and real encampments of soldiers. The Channel waters off the phantom headquarters at Dover and nearby rivers were convincingly crowded with ghostly fleets of dummy landing craft, indistinguishable from the real thing to German observation planes.

Meanwhile, farther west along the Channel, British and American army and navy units began rehearsals for the strike to come. At Slapton Sands and Lyme Beach, ships, planes, landing craft, tanks, and men ran through the motions of landing against simulated enemy resistance. In one tragic case, a landing drill ran into prowling German torpedo boats. In the short, bitter, and confused action that followed, 638 Allied soldiers and sailors lost their lives.

But the Germans continued to bite on the Pas-de-Calais bait. May weather had been perfect for invasion, and the defenders were fully alert. Now, May was running out, and the Germans reasoned that an invasion would be held off to coincide with the beginning of the expected Russian offensive on the eastern front. Weather conditions there would not be ripe until late June.

Ever so slightly, German vigilance relaxed. On June 4, Field Marshal Rommel decided to go home for a short visit to celebrate his wife's birthday; Frau Rommel had been born on the sixth of June.

By then, the time had been set for the invasion. Operation Overlord, code name for the European offensive, was scheduled for June 5; all preparations were geared to that date.

As against the tiny forces available when he arrived in England in June of 1942, General Eisenhower now had at his disposal seventeen British Empire divisions, twenty American divisions, one Free French division, and one Free Polish division— more than 600,000 men all told— plus 10,000 combat planes, 5,000 transport planes and gliders, and some 5,000 seaborne craft, from battleships to sailing vessels.

There were flurries of last-minute

The Atlantic Wall's defenses included radar installations to warn of an invasion fleet approaching across the Channel.

A low-flying Allied plane, photographing beach obstacles in Normandy, sends German workmen scurrying for cover.

20

A German artist painted this view of a casemated coastal battery under construction. Inland defenses were stripped of their guns to strengthen the Atlantic Wall.

decisions and disagreements. British air commanders took a dim view of the American insistence on paratroop drops in major strength. They estimated losses up to eighty per cent. But top-level planners insisted that the air drops were essential, and General Eisenhower endorsed their judgment with a heavy heart.

It remained only for the final command to be given. And then a heavy storm blew up in the Atlantic.

There was a hurried meeting on Saturday evening, June 3, to hear a forecast of stormy weather. Another meeting was set for four o'clock the next morning. The weather still looked ominous, and Eisenhower was faced with a choice. He could either attempt Overlord one day late despite the weather, or because of the need to wait for another favorable tide period on the French coast, he could postpone the operation for at least two weeks.

Some units were already at sea at the time of this briefing. Eisenhower decided to cancel the June 5 invasion date and wait twenty-four hours to see if the weather would permit an assault on the sixth. Since strict radio silence was already in effect, the only way of turning back some of the ships was to intercept them at sea. There were anxious hours as one troop convoy was missed by the three destroyers sent out to notify it and was only reached at last by an ancient British seaplane.

On Sunday night, June 4, the plan-

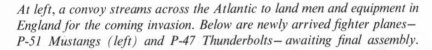

At left, a convoy streams across the Atlantic to land men and equipment in England for the coming invasion. Below are newly arrived fighter planes— P-51 Mustangs (left) and P-47 Thunderbolts— awaiting final assembly.

U.S. ARMY

23

ners met again. A high wind shrieked outside, and rain lashed the headquarters' windows. In spite of this, the weathermen predicted that the storm was breaking up and that by June 6 conditions would be much improved. While the high command wrestled with the problem, the convoys were sent out again— subject to recall.

As the final deadline approached, the generals and the admirals had their say; then the meeting fell silent. The final decision and responsibility were General Eisenhower's alone. At 4:15 on Monday morning he said briskly, "O. K. We'll go." He had accepted the gamble and chosen to launch the invasion only one day late. Tuesday, the sixth of June, was to be D-Day.

In the nervous hours of June 5, General Eisenhower prepared for the worst, writing on a slip of paper an announcement he hoped he would never have to make: "Our landings in the Cherbourg-Havre area have failed to gain a satisfactory foothold and I have withdrawn the troops. . . . The troops, the air, and the Navy did all that bravery and devotion to duty could do. If any blame or fault attaches to the attempt it is mine alone." He shoved the paper into a jacket pocket. He was too busy for the next

In April and May of 1944 full-scale invasion rehearsals took place; shown here is the exercise at Slapton Sands, on the coast of southern England. Live ammunition made these maneuvers realistic and dangerous.

A D-DAY GLOSSARY

D-Day is a military term signifying, for purposes of advance planning, the unknown date in the future when an attack will be launched. By common usage it has come to stand for the 1944 invasion of Normandy.

H-Hour, another term of military convenience, is the hour on D-Day that the operation begins. Because of differing tidal conditions, H-Hour for the three Normandy assault areas varied by as much as eighty-five minutes.

Overlord was the code name for the entire Allied campaign to invade and liberate France and Western Europe.

Neptune stood for the first phase of Overlord: the planning of the Normandy assault, the movement of the immense armada across the English Channel, and the battle for the beaches.

The Atlantic Wall, Germany's first line of defense in the west, lay along the Channel coast of France. Only partly completed by June, 1944, it consisted of fortified gun emplacements, beach obstacles, and mine fields. The part of the Wall directly opposite England was manned by Field Marshal Rommel's Seventh and Fifteenth armies, containing thirty-seven divisions.

Landing Craft used in the invasion were mainly of six types. The LCVP (Landing Craft Vehicle & Personnel) ferried ashore a thirty-two man combat team or a small vehicle. The British equivalent was the LCA (Landing Craft Assault), an armored wooden craft. These assault craft were carried across the Channel aboard troop transports. The 158-foot seagoing LCI (Landing Craft Infantry) delivered some two hundred troops directly onto the beach. Heavy weapons and tanks were delivered by LSTs (Landing Ship Tank), 327 feet long and costing $1,500,000 apiece; 229 of them were used in the invasion. LCTs (Landing Craft Tank) and LCMs (Landing Craft Mechanized) ferried tanks and guns ashore.

Infantry formed the backbone of both the attacking and defending forces on D-Day. An American infantry division contained 14,037 men, divided into three regiments (with three battalions in each regiment), plus an additional four battalions of artillery, and miscellaneous units (medics, engineers, etc.). A German infantry division was smaller (12,769 men), but had somewhat greater firepower.

Artillery to support the Allied landings came mainly from warships, ranging from the 5-inch guns of destroyers to the great 15-inch batteries of the British battleships *Warspite* and *Ramillies*. German coastal batteries were thus often outgunned; the Fort St. Marcouf battery, for instance, mounted three 210-millimeter guns firing shells about eight inches in diameter. Of the German artillery trained on the beaches themselves, probably the most dangerous was the versatile 88-millimeter (about 3½-inch) gun, used both as an antitank and antiaircraft weapon.

six weeks to remember the note's existence. When he found it then, it had become history that never happened.

The troops quartered near Dover— the only real part of General Patton's phantom army— stole silently into trucks and then into transport craft. A handful of men left behind kept cookhouse fires going and moved trucks back and forth in the deserted encampment to keep up the ruse.

Air cover for the true assault began at nine o'clock the evening of June 5. For the next twenty-four hours the skies above southern England were a solid hum of menacing sound. All up and down the English coast civilian ears were cocked to the ceaseless beat of propellers. The invasion of Fortress Europe was under way.

The storm had abated. In its stead was a dreary drizzle of chill rain that spattered the strained faces of men on thousands of ships.

American infantrymen, in full battle dress, were sketched by a combat artist as they waited on the English coast for General Eisenhower's signal to launch the invasion.

In this panoramic painting by a British artist, tanks and ambulances move into the gaping hull of an LST (center). Part of the invasion armada lies offshore.

2.

Crossing the Channel

While Overlord was the over-all title for the liberation of France, the complex operations for carrying out the Normandy landings were lumped under the code name Neptune. Neptune is a more apt word for the vital role of the Allied navies in the assault.

Even under the best of conditions, it would have been no simple task to transport some 200,000 fighting men and all their equipment from scattered ports on the English coast to the beaches of France in less than twenty-four hours. A determined enemy had done his skillful best to multiply this basic transport problem.

The English Channel was sown with deadly mines and patrolled by naval units; manning the beach fortifications were anxious and indeed desperate troops equipped with everything from heavy artillery to machine guns. The Luftwaffe (the German Air Force) posed a threat in the air. Finally, there was the Channel weather, dangerously changeable and quite capable of upsetting the best-laid plans.

While they tried to keep German attention focused on the Pas-de-Calais opposite Dover, the invasion planners cast their eyes on the Normandy coast to the west. They chose the area lying between the Orne River and the Cotentin Peninsula.

Three simultaneous landings were to be made. The base of the Cotentin Peninsula was designated as Utah Beach, the assignment of the United States VII Corps. About fifteen miles

The "invasion funnel" for Operation Neptune is outlined in the shaded area of this map. Piccadilly Circus was the hub where Allied ships converged before proceeding through the lanes cleared by mine sweepers to the five Normandy invasion beaches. The Germans had been misled into expecting an attack on the Pas-de-Calais (upper right).

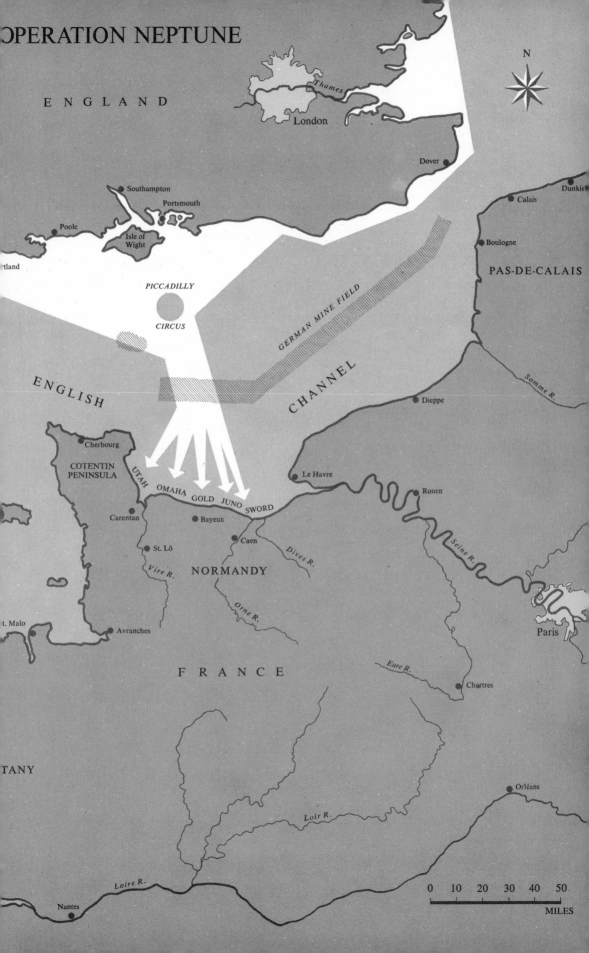

to the east, facing the town of St. Laurent, was the longer stretch labeled Omaha Beach, the target of the United States V Corps. Farther east, running all the way from Arromanches to the mouth of the Orne, lay the three British beaches, Gold, Juno, and Sword.

Naval preparations for Neptune had begun in February, 1944, under British Admiral Sir Bertram Ramsay's direction. Rivalries between the American and the British services were quickly buried under the immense pressure of putting together what Admiral Ramsay (explaining the fact that his orders covered 1,100 printed pages) described accurately as "the largest and most complicated operation ever undertaken."

Up until almost the last moment, there was a continuing demand for more warships. The United States Navy, already busily occupied in the Pacific, was hard put to spare heavy support for the invasion of France. Three venerable battleships— *Arkansas, Nevada,* and *Texas*— were made available, plus three cruisers and thirty-one destroyers, a division of which arrived only days before D-Day.

The Royal Navy supplied the bulk of the vital gunfire support— three battleships, seventeen cruisers, thirty-seven destroyers, and a monitor, or

On the night of June 5 the English Channel swarmed with thousands of Allied ships. The column of landing craft at center, jammed with tanks and guns for the great battle ahead, stretches toward the horizon.

33

floating battery. The British also furnished most of the mine sweepers and other small craft especially designed for invasion chores.

The official listing of the ships involved in Neptune resembled a telephone directory. The Utah Beach task force, for example, included 743 vessels, from the battleship *Nevada* through numerous types of landing craft down to dozens of torpedo-carrying PT-boats. Tacked on at the end of the list was a miscellany of coasters, barges, and even sailing ships. All of this was for just one of the three assault targets and did not include craft involved in ventures like the artificial harbors and breakwaters.

Landing craft presented perhaps the biggest headache throughout all the planning for D-Day. Landing craft priorities had been shifted from the European Theater to the Pacific in 1942, when it became obvious that no immediate cross-Channel assault would occur. Then, after the invasion had been set for 1944, it was difficult to get the Pacific planners to release their hard-won craft. There were also differences between the British and American estimates of how many men could be carried by different types of landing craft.

It was February, 1944, before the high command was able to make any order out of the conflicting needs and estimates. Even so, the invasion was postponed from May to June to allow another month's production of landing craft to reach England from American shipyards. It was all so confusing and frustrating that at a top-level planning conference Prime Minister Winston Churchill grumbled, "The destinies of two great empires . . . seem to be tied up in some God-damned things called LSTs. . . ."

But now it was June, and all the LSTs—and LCIs and LCVPs and LCAs and LCMs—were crammed to capacity with invading GIs and their weapons, ready to slip out into the doubtful weather from every conceivable port and harbor and river mouth along the coast of southern England. The operation would resemble a huge funnel, its mouth the 250 miles of British coast line, its narrow neck extending from about mid-Channel to the fifty-mile stretch of Normandy beaches.

The D-Day date had to take into consideration not only weather, but time and tide as well. For the sake of secrecy, the vast body of troops had to cross the Channel under cover of darkness; to hit the beaches effectively required at least the first light of dawn.

Tide conditions must be just right—low enough to permit the landing craft to ground and discharge the troops in shallow water, yet high enough on the beaches to shorten the dash across open sands controlled by enemy guns. The Army argued for high tide, the Navy for low. The final compromise called for H-Hour (the precise time of landing) shortly after low tide between June 5 and June 7. On these three days, favorable tide conditions would be repeated later the same day to allow reinforcements to be landed.

The Germans had made the Channel an unpredictable salt-water booby trap from Brest to Calais, but their mine-laying operation was not as effective as it could have been. Admiral Theodor Krancke had U-boats and torpedo boats to patrol the Channel, but the Admiral considered early June an unlikely invasion period; his scouting patrols were not even out on the crucial night.

Much the same casual philosophy governed the planting of the German mine fields. Their free-floating mines had timers to flood and sink them after a certain period so that they would not drift too far and endanger supposedly safe German shipping routes. A whole undersea curtain of mines had been laid in the Channel, but the larger part was useless by June

Scottish Highlanders aboard a troop transport got a few badly needed laughs from a booklet telling them where to go and what to see when they arrived in France.

when German military minds felt a spring invasion threat would be over.

More dangerous were "oyster" mines, which could be sown from the air. These mines lay on the sea floor and would explode at the changing water pressure caused by an approaching ship. Only another stroke of good fortune saved Neptune from the oysters. A plentiful supply had been stored near the Channel ready for use. But the Luftwaffe's Reichsmarshal Hermann Goering, fearful that the invaders would quickly overrun the supply depot, had the mines removed to greater safety inland instead of solving his problem by planting them in the Channel.

None of this meant that the Channel was clear of mines laid in previous German defense operations, and mine sweepers were the first units to go into action. British and American sweepers began their ticklish task in the last days of May. The whole invasion funnel had not only to be swept clean, but swept so as to give the enemy no inkling of the invasion route.

The mine sweepers cleared lanes to the ten-mile circle in the Channel nicknamed Piccadilly Circus, where the troop convoys would meet to enter the narrowing neck of the funnel. From Piccadilly Circus, the sweepers then cut lanes toward the different beaches through the main German mine field lying off the Normandy coast.

The sweepers were followed by spe-

At dawn on June 6, the British battleships Ramillies *and* Warspite *opened a fierce two-hour bombardment of German coastal batteries in the English invasion area. The two sturdy old ships continued to support the troops ashore all during D-Day.*

cial craft that dropped small buoys to mark the safe sea lanes. Near the beaches the number of lanes increased from five to ten to allow separate passage of slow and fast convoys. The traffic pattern became as complicated as midtown New York on a rainy day.

This preliminary clearing went along with no major mishaps, but there were a few close calls. Bad weather complicated the job. A Royal Navy mine sweeping flotilla was trying to clean up a dangerous field on the morning of June 4 when the destroyer H. M. S. *Campbell*, approaching to tell the

sweepers the invasion had been postponed a day, floundered into the middle of the mined waters. The sweepers managed to explode enough of the mines so that the *Campbell* escaped undamaged.

The mine sweepers and buoy ships would have to repeat their dangerous operations on D-Day to be sure no stray mines had drifted into the lanes; they would also have to sweep right up to the beaches themselves.

The troops already at sea for the original June 5 date spent a wet and seasick period of misery marking time

37

The American mine sweeper Tide *(center) helped clear the sea lanes for D-Day. She is seen here on June 7, after being blasted by an enemy mine. For security reasons, the photograph was retouched to blot out the radar antennae on the ships' masts.*

when the invasion date was changed. The other ships waited in harbors as soaked GIs tried to forget their nervousness by telling each other jokes, playing cards, or thinking about home. The mine sweepers steamed out again as the hour of embarkation approached. Then the final signal came, and the great unwieldy armada stirred and began to move out into the Channel. The dice were cast in the greatest gamble of World War II; at stake was the liberation of Europe.

No military plan has ever been made with more care or in greater detail. Yet the combination of water, wind, weather, and darkness, and the varying reactions of thousands of human beings to intense danger, made mixups inevitable.

In Lewis Carroll's *Alice in Wonderland,* the Mock Turtle cries, "There's a

38

porpoise close behind us, and he's treading on my tail," an apt description of what happened on that fateful night. The heaving, wallowing landing craft, hard to steer even in calm water, seemed to climb on each other's backs. Land-loving infantrymen from Kansas City and Denver and Nottingham turned various shades of green in the crowded darkness. Others shouted insults or encouragement to the troops in passing craft to keep their spirits up.

Yet, thanks to superb seamanship— and an assist from Lady Luck—the vast flotilla held its course. Hundreds upon hundreds of ships converged at Piccadilly Circus in the Channel, managed the giant traffic turn toward the beach targets, and lumbered along the lanes cleared by the mine sweepers.

It was one of the mine sweepers, the *Osprey*, that became the first naval casualty of the operation. She struck a mine neglected in previous sweeps and took a gaping hole in her forward engine room. Fires got out of control. Six men were lost, and the *Osprey* was abandoned to sink at 6:15 on the evening of June 5.

The sweepers continued on to the very edge of the Normandy coastal waters. Naval firepower followed them. The cruiser *Augusta*, with United States Rear Admiral Alan G. Kirk aboard, led the task forces headed for Utah and Omaha beaches. Rear Admiral Sir Philip Vian on the cruiser *Scylla* spearheaded the British movement toward Gold, Sword, and Juno beaches. Battleships, cruisers, destroy-ers, and other combat craft made up this vanguard; after them trailed the endless numbers of landing craft, packed like sardine cans with troops and more troops.

By midnight of the fifth of June, the heavy naval support ships were in position, lying silent and watchful off the coast. The mine sweepers moved closer to the shore, marking safe lanes. A long, winding trail of assault craft stubbornly kept course behind each of them. It seemed to the men in the invading fleet that the whole Channel was alive with ships and men. They could not understand the absence of activity from the enemy.

At about 3:00 A.M. German radar finally picked up the invasion fleet, and the word was relayed to Admiral Krancke. He ordered out his sparse naval forces—submarines, destroyers, and torpedo boats. The shore batteries were told to hold their fire until it became light enough to estimate the enemy's strength and position.

The first German artillery fire began before the last mine sweepers were through with their work. Big guns took aim at the United States destroyers *Corry* and *Fitch* off Utah Beach. Shore batteries farther east menaced mine sweepers working toward the beaches. H.M.S. *Black Prince* returned the fire to distract attention from the sweepers.

OVERLEAF: *From an attack transport anchored off the Normandy coast, American infantrymen scramble down a loading net into the LCVP that will carry them ashore.*

The last long battle for Europe was joined.

The German fire came uncomfortably close to the warships off Utah, and Rear Admiral Morton L. Deyo decided to advance the timing of the naval bombardment. The cruisers *Tuscaloosa*, *Black Prince*, and *Hawkins* and the battleship *Nevada* began firing heavy, thundering barrages from offshore; at the same time, Allied planes laid a smoke screen to shield the Utah Beach vessels from enemy observation.

The destroyer *Corry* failed to get this protective screen in time, and the German guns concentrated on her. Maneuvering to escape their fire, she struck a mine that knocked out her power. Within minutes she was sinking. Sister ships saved most of the *Corry*'s crew, but thirteen were killed and thirty-three wounded.

Off Omaha and the three British beaches similar gun duels were being waged. Then the first landing craft pushed their blunt, ugly noses onto French soil. Under German fire, the infantrymen scrambled out to seek a footing in the wet sand.

The men struggling for a toehold on the smoky, shell-torn beaches were not the first to breach Hitler's *Festung Europa*. Miles inland, thousands of invaders had dropped from the dark sky and were fighting for their lives.

In the ominous gray light of early morning, an assault craft idles offshore awaiting H-Hour, the tension of the moment reflected in the faces of the men crouched inside.

43

B-26 Marauder bombers take off from an English airfield to support the D-Day landings. All Allied planes were painted with black and white stripes for easy identification in the crowded air over Normandy.

3.

Invasion from the Air

One overpowering memory common to almost every man who participated in D-Day was the sight and sound of the planes that stretched like a dark cloud across the Channel sky. From dawn to dusk they were always there, a constant and comforting reminder of the immense power behind the Allied invasion.

The aerial softening up of German defenses had begun long before D-Day. It was carefully planned to pile heavy explosives into the proposed landing areas without giving the Germans a clue as to where the invaders would strike. As a result, for every raid near the Normandy beaches, three other targets along the French coast were plastered by the bombers. It was all part of the vital lesson the Allies had learned— command of the air was absolutely essential for a successful invasion in modern warfare.

From the beginning of 1944, air bombardment increased not only in intensity, but also in the destruction of specific targets tied in with the invasion planning. It was going to be hard enough to win a position on the beaches of Normandy; it would be impossible to do so if the Germans were able to bring strong reinforcements of men, tanks, and artillery into the critical area. Bombing raids had to aim at sealing off the landing beaches from these German reserves inland.

The Allies ran the risk that this heavy bombing might turn the French people against them. Even though the eventual goal was liberation, it would have been understandable for them to feel anger at the planes which destroyed their cities and, however accidentally, killed their families and their friends.

But the French, with many wars behind them, and with an abiding hatred for their German conquerors, took bombing in their stride. General Eisenhower wrote that "far from being alienated, [they] accepted the hardships and suffering with a realism worthy of a farsighted nation." They did more than merely accept; Free French underground resistance groups sabotaged roads and railway lines.

The major air offensive began in April. It was thorough and effective, spreading its damage far beyond the obvious routes to and from Normandy and never letting the Germans guess the pattern of the invasion to come. Bridge after bridge was cut down by aerial bombing. By late May, all the rail lines and highways crossing the Seine River west of Paris ended abruptly at the riverbank; it would take the Germans more than a month to put them in working order.

Bombing closer to the beaches was lighter to preserve security, but it still slashed German rail traffic by one-third. In one day alone, fighter-bombers destroyed fifty locomotives near the Cotentin Peninsula and severely damaged sixty-three others elsewhere in France.

Another prime target in Normandy was a cluster of deadly German 170-millimeter guns. They had a range of eighteen miles and were so mobile that the Germans seldom fired more than two shells from the same spot. Allied Intelligence officers spotted eight of them; all eight were knocked out by the prowling fighter-bombers.

Yet all of this was petty compared to the thousands of planes that filled the sky for the invasion itself. D-Day air activity got under way the evening of June 5, while ships were still loading their cargoes of men and guns. For the

first twenty-four hours of the invasion, an average of over one thousand Allied aircraft were in the air every hour. Fighters raked the beaches, bombers pounded German supply lines and storage depots inland, and special planes spotted targets for naval guns or laid protective smoke screens.

There were also units of airborne invaders to land, by parachute or by glider, behind the German beach defenses even before the first water-borne invaders were in sight of land. Theirs was perhaps the greatest gamble of a gambling day and one of the most chaotic yet successful parts of the invasion.

The British 6th Airborne Division had as its target an area covering twenty-five square miles, with its key objectives the bridges over the Dives and Orne rivers. The Dives is a small river flowing near Caen, the principal city toward which the British landings were directed. The Orne, a larger river, flows through Caen to the Channel.

The British airborne units were to destroy the Dives bridges, thus cutting off German reinforcements that might be used against the landings. At the same time, they were to save one bridge over the Orne and another bridge over a nearby canal to keep open a line of communication between their own forces and the beach invaders. The whole plan depended on split-second timing, on each airborne wave succeeding in its mission and clearing the way for the wave to follow.

The first drops, aimed at capturing

A major objective of the Allied air campaign was to disable the Normandy railroad system. The photograph above was taken from a fighter-bomber as it shot up a German supply train. The Loire River bridge below was knocked out by bombers.

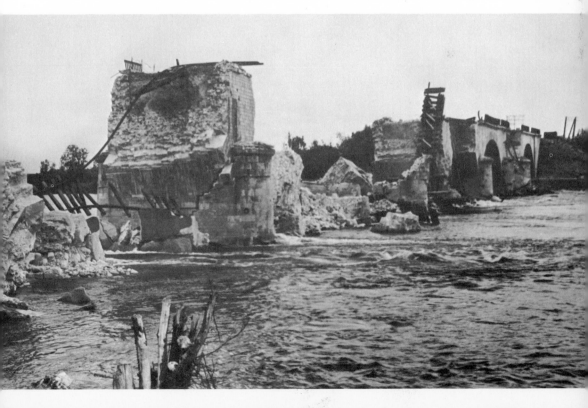

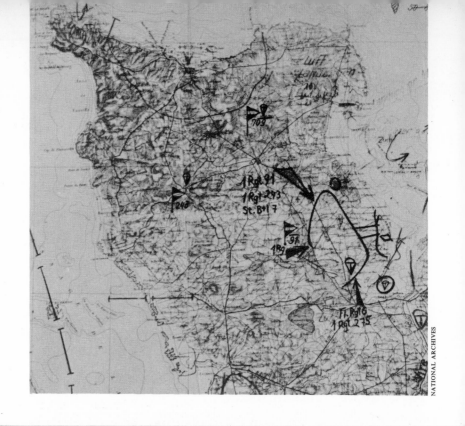

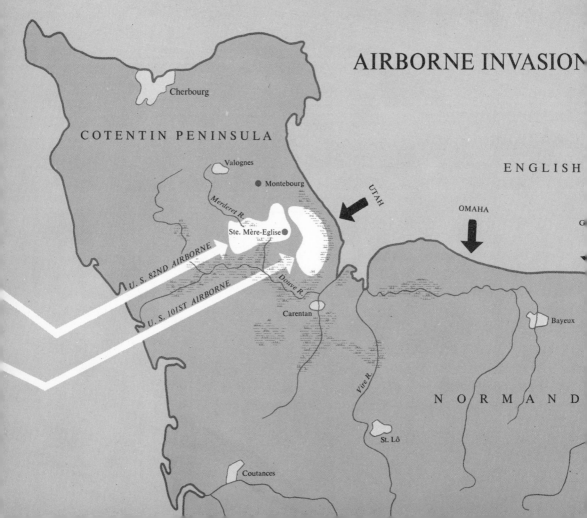

AIRBORNE INVASION

Cherbourg

COTENTIN PENINSULA

Valognes

Montebourg

Merderet R.

Ste. Mère-Eglise

UTAH

ENGLISH

OMAHA

U. S. 82ND AIRBORNE

U. S. 101ST AIRBORNE

Douve R.

Carentan

Bayeux

Vire R.

NORMAND

St. Lô

Coutances

The shaded portions of the map below—largely flooded marshland—show where the bulk of the U.S. and British airborne forces landed. Some paratroopers and gliders were scattered far and wide outside these areas. The U.S. 82nd and 101st divisions sealed off the Utah beachhead; the British 6th Airborne secured the right flank at Sword Beach. The arrows on the captured German field map at left indicate initial enemy moves against the American drop zone behind Utah.

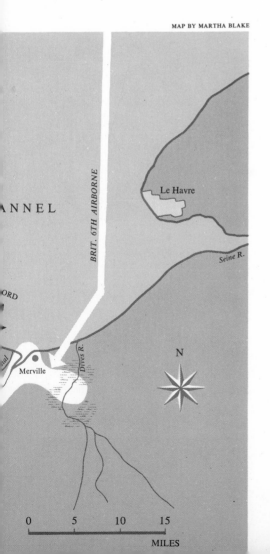

intact the Orne and the canal bridges, were brilliantly successful. In the darkness, one glider scudded across the ground at ninety miles an hour, sliding to a stop less than twenty yards from its target; troops tumbled out of gaping holes in the fuselage and, in three minutes, took the canal bridge from its bewildered German guards.

Hunting horns summoned other dropped troops to assemble. The Germans, braced for the usual bombing and strafing raids, were caught unprepared. British troops swarmed past the defenses, disconnected the wires to explosives with which the Germans had planned to destroy the Orne bridge, and secured that objective.

Later drops ran into more confusion and trouble. Field Marshal Rommel had not neglected the possibility of an airborne invasion in his defensive measures. Barbed wire, explosive booby traps, and most dangerous of all, controlled flooding of the flatlands around the Dives had turned a large portion of the British target area into a boggy death trap. Seven-foot-deep ditches, slimy with mud and water, cut through the lowlands in a zigzag maze. The heavily loaded paratroops who tumbled into them often drowned at once; at best, they had a long and painful struggle before they could regain dry land and make an effort to rejoin their units and find their objectives.

Paratroops who jumped from transport planes that had missed their targets plummeted into strange territory and could find none of the expected landmarks to guide them. Some pilots got the Orne and the Dives rivers mixed up and dropped their troops into deadly marshlands. But surprise was still on the Allied side. The Germans simply did not know how many men were landing or where.

When Lieutenant Colonel Terence Otway of the British 6th Airborne tumbled to the ground, he could find only some of his troops, and most of them were dazed or exhausted after struggling in the oozing swampland.

With only 150 men, he set out for the crucially important Nazi shore battery at Merville, where the Orne meets the Channel just east of the British landing area.

Plans for taking the Merville battery called for glider-borne reinforcements, but Colonel Otway watched helplessly as the gliders passed by overhead— the flares with which he was to signal them that the assault was under way had been lost in the drop. It was now 4:30 A.M. In forty-five minutes,

These pictures were taken in the British airborne sector. Above, casualties are evacuated across the Caen Canal bridge on the afternoon of D-Day. The night before, the bridge was captured intact by troops who landed in the gliders in the background. At left is a command post in a field near Caen. In the German photograph below, an enemy soldier examines a British glider that has been shot down.

unless it received word that the battery had been captured, the Navy would turn its big guns on the area. Undaunted, Otway ordered his skimpy force of paratroopers to attack.

The German defense was hot and heavy. The British rushed through uncleared mine fields and hurled themselves against the battery. Hugging the concrete walls, they fired at the German garrison through the gun openings in the casemates. So much equipment had been lost in the drop that the British, once they had battered their way inside the fortifications, had to use German shells to blow up the guns.

There were only seventy-five men left of the 150 who had charged the battery. They found a flare to signal the capture, and it was spotted by a plane which relayed the word to the Royal Navy only fifteen minutes before the bombardment was to begin. A carrier pigeon, rumpled and much the worse for having spent hours tucked into a signal officer's shirt, flew back to England with the message that the Merville battery was no longer a threat.

Other drops were scattered all over and far beyond the target area, yet somehow enough men came together to achieve their objectives. The five bridges over the Dives were effectively blown up. Some units met at dawn

Many American paratroopers had their hair cut in Iroquois scalp locks for the D-Day air drops. These men of the 101st Airborne Division, the "Screaming Eagles," completed the effect by daubing each other with war paint.

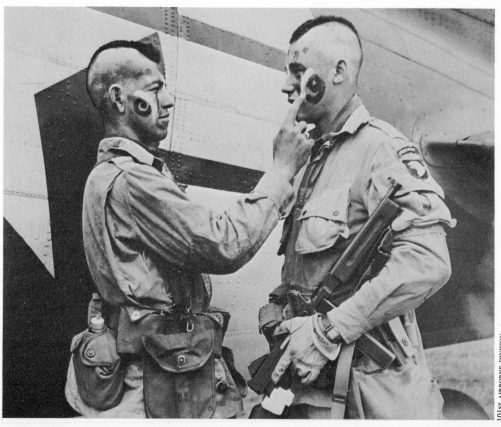

with only one man out of ten accounted for. Actual casualties were not this high, but it would be days before stray paratroopers, lost and keeping under cover behind enemy lines, found their way back to their own forces.

The twenty-five square miles of planned objective were under shaky British control, even though larger German forces lay all around them. Many of the gliders carrying antitank guns and vehicles had been smashed or shot down, but enough found their way safely to earth to halt German counterattacks.

The American paratroopers had two separate drop areas. The 101st Airborne Division, under Major General Maxwell D. Taylor, was to win control of the approaches to the Utah Beach area and cut off German reinforcements from Carentan to the south. Major General Matthew B. Ridgeway's 82nd Airborne was to land near Ste. Mère-Eglise to secure that town and to provide protection against enemy action from the northwest.

Both drops were muddled by bad visibility and antiaircraft fire, but the Americans, like the British, were saved by the combination of German surprise and the doggedness and courage of the men who fell from the skies.

The Germans, even as the invaders landed behind their lines, stuck stubbornly to their theory that the main assault would be launched in the Pas-de-Calais area farther east. Ranking officers insisted that the air drops were only diversions designed to distract attention from the real danger point.

At the same time, the Germans believed that the landing forces were much larger than they were. As with the British air drop, the American sector was laced with misguided gliders and paratroopers (some units landed ten miles from their proper targets), giving the impression of a truly mammoth air invasion. If the Germans had known the real strength of the airborne troops, they might easily have diverted enough men to wipe out the whole operation before morning.

The 101st Airborne consisted of three parachute regiments and one glider regiment. Their target area covered marshy ground between Ste. Mère-Eglise and the shore. What was not known, and what turned out to be nearly disastrous, was that much of the land marked "soft" on maps was in fact deep water. The German policy of defensive flooding was in effect in this section, too.

Nobody knows the exact number of men who drowned on landing. There are no accurate statistics for the chaotic airborne assaults. But again and again survivors reported seeing their fellow soldiers, weighted down by parachute harness and heavy equipment, disappear into the uncharted pools. The luckier and stronger men were able to unbuckle their harnesses and half-swim, half-wade to safety. The luckiest of all landed on solid earth, but even they had their troubles.

A nervous German patrol, sent by an officer to find out what was going

At dusk on June 5, heavily laden American paratroopers march onto an airfield in England to board the C-47 transport planes that will carry them over Normandy.

on, stumbled upon three lost American paratroopers, one of them seriously injured. The Germans were startled to see emblazoned on the jackets of the cocky invaders a pin-up girl and the hopeful slogan, "See You in Paris." They disarmed their prisoners and then helped care for the wounded jumper. However, he was beyond aid and died within minutes. The dark inferno of war was forgotten for a moment as the Germans joined with the two Americans in saying the Lord's Prayer over the body. Then the captors herded their two prisoners back to the German command post.

Men who dropped in or near Ste. Mère-Eglise fell into what must have seemed like the mouth of hell. The Germans were blazing away at the scores of transport planes and parachutes faintly visible in the dark sky. Twenty Americans miscarried into the town itself, and on them the German

garrison spent all its rage and surprised fury. A single paratrooper who landed in a tree near the town square drew submachine-gun fire from half a dozen Germans until his riddled corpse hung swaying from its lines.

The total area of the American drop zones was wider than that of the British, and the scattering of troops due to navigational errors, wind drift, and misjudgment was even greater. A major problem of both the 101st and

C-47s are shown towing three of the 867 gliders used in the invasion across the English Channel. Glider-borne infantry and artillery provided badly needed support for the paratroopers who were fighting behind German lines. The ships churning toward France carry reinforcements to the beaches.

the 82nd divisions on D-Day eve was simply sorting themselves out and finding where they were.

One of their objectives, near St. Martin-de-Varreville, was a big German battery. It commanded an important exit from Utah Beach and had been heavily bombed from the air, but nobody knew whether it was still in operation. Captain Frank Lillyman, the first American soldier to touch the soil of Normandy, scouted the site and found that the air strike had put the battery out of action. But the whole back-beach area still remained to be cleared for the landing forces. Roads had either to be blocked to German reinforcements or kept open to allow the beach troops to move inland. Hard, tough, slow battling was ahead, all of it with forces scattered in strange terrain, with equipment lost, and with the men frequently cut off from any commanding officer.

It was a group of seventeen captured paratroopers who helped turn the tide at Foucarville. The prisoners were held in the fortified German position on a hill outside the town. They were disarmed and helpless, but they still had a strong weapon— rumor. They told the Germans that the hill was to be the target for a major bombardment at 10:30 on the night of June 6. The rumor spread, and with it, uneasiness.

The defenders held on all day against paratroopers reinforced by airborne

These American soldiers were killed before they had a chance to fire a shot at the enemy. Their glider crashed and flipped over as it attempted a landing in a Normandy field.

glider groups, but as 10:30 neared, their nerve broke. A group of them made a dash to escape, and the prisoners snatched up their abandoned weapons. The Americans surrounding the position suddenly saw their opposition fall apart, with one detachment of Germans coming downhill to surrender, another dashing northward, and between them a tiny body of paratroopers happily firing at the fleeing enemy.

The same story of confusion and recovery was repeated again and again. Brigadier General James A. Gavin, second in command of the 82nd, hit French earth in an orchard full of cows. He tried to make his way out and find his men along what seemed to be a long, shallow lake unmarked on any map. The "lake" turned out to be the dammed-up Merderet River, shown on the planning maps as a narrow stream no wider than a New England creek.

General Gavin began his D-Day mission in command of less than twenty men, and even by morning he had been able to pull together only 150 troops from dozens of different units. With this force he tried for one important objective, the capture of a bridge over the Merderet. A powerful German counterattack with tanks upset this scheme, but Gavin and his men were at least able to keep the enemy from using this approach to the Utah beachhead.

Ste. Mère-Eglise, after its first fatal reception of the invaders from the air, had a happier ending. The German garrison was badly rattled. The 505th Parachute Regiment made the most accurate of all the American drops, less than a mile northwest of the town. Two battalions quickly assembled and moved on Ste. Mère-Eglise while enemy confusion was at its height. They took the town and ran up an American flag already blooded in successful paratroop actions in Italy. The huge swastika that had dominated the town square for four long years came down for good. Ste. Mère-Eglise was the first French town to fall to the Allies.

To the east, well-laid plans to cut off a bridge across the Douve River dissolved in a tangle of confusion. Lieutenant Colonel Thomas Shanley pulled together a small force and scouted the area. He discovered the enemy firmly established at Picauville, but fortunately they were not disposed to move out and strike against the airborne invaders.

This lack of flexibility, one result of the rigid discipline in the German Army, saved the paratroopers time and again through the long night of the air drops. Where the invaders landed precisely on or near German defense units, enemy reaction was fierce and effective. But at no time during the first hours is there any record of Germans taking the initiative to move against the paratroopers, even when (as frequently happened) they had a commanding superiority in men and weapons.

Shanley led skirmishers close to

Picauville and, on his way, picked up an additional force of two hundred Americans which he discovered sitting in a meadow waiting for some kind of direction. Even with this reinforcement, the Douve bridge target was impossible. French citizens confirmed the strength of the Germans at Picauville (three infantry companies, an artillery battery, and four tanks) and added that nearby Etienville was even more strongly garrisoned.

Shanley made the only decision possible and settled for occupying a hill near the Merderet River. His men were the farthest inland of all the drops; they would be cut off and in serious danger for two full days before the territory was brought under American control.

Of all the acts of heroism on that fateful day, none shines more brightly than the exploit of Sergeant Harrison Summers and Private John Camin of the 101st Airborne. They took on a German garrison stationed back of Utah Beach. At first by himself, and later with Camin's help, Summers stormed one fortress-like stone barracks after another, kicking in the doors and cutting down the defenders with submachine-gun fire. Eventually, they had ten buildings to their credit and had accounted for at least seventy-five Germans killed or captured.

By sunrise on June 6, an irregular space some fifty miles long and five miles across, two to five miles inland from the Utah Beach area, was an ant

heap of scurrying American airborne troops— some lost, some joined together haphazardly in small units, some organized for effective action. Wrecked and abandoned gliders were scattered about, and jeeps and weapons lay broken or half-sunk in the flooded marshes.

Most exit roads from Utah were controlled by American paratroopers. Ste. Mère-Eglise had been taken, and equally important, the German defense system had been thrown into a damaging state of uncertainty. German forces well behind the Utah Beach sector were heavily occupied with American paratroopers who seemed to pop up at every turn. Essential routes back of Gold, Sword, and Juno beaches were under the control of the British 6th Airborne Division.

The Luftwaffe was almost nonexistent as an enemy, and throughout the daylight hours and into D-Day night, new strings of gliders continued to pour in reinforcements to the paratroop detachments behind the coast line.

Four days later, Field Marshal Rommel, in a report to his superiors, testified to the success of Allied air power and still overestimated the power of the airborne assault. "Our operations in Normandy," the Ger-

Circling transports release gliders near Ste. Mère-Eglise on the morning of June 7. The small Normandy fields, tightly boxed in by embankments and thick hedges, were the scene of scores of disastrous glider crashes.

man commander wrote, "are tremendously hampered, and in some places even rendered impossible by . . . the immensely powerful, at times overwhelming, superiority of the enemy air force. . . . Parachute and airborne troops are employed in such numbers and with such flexibility that the troops they engage are hard put to it to fight them off. Where they drop into territory not held by our troops, they dig in immediately and can no longer be dislodged. . . . Our situation is becoming extremely difficult."

American and British airborne troops, hiding behind hedges and in ditches, cut off from each other and often from the landmarks they had expected to find, did not have the comfort of knowing all this. Nor, fortunately, did Rommel know that at least part of the vast "flexibility" he feared had come from landing errors and misplaced drops.

There were no rules in the bitter, savage battle behind the beaches. There was little information about what was happening or where or why. There was only the need to play it by ear, to form and reform units, to strike and fight and hold, and to hope that all the death and confusion was playing its vital part in the grand gamble by helping pave the way for the men who were hitting the beaches.

Edging warily past the bodies of comrades killed by German snipers, American airborne troops advance on Carentan. The town fell a week after D-Day, following a savage battle.

63

4.
Utah Beachhead

This picture was taken shortly after H-Hour at Utah Beach. Protected by the guns of the amphibious tanks in the background, infantry pours ashore unopposed. The man in the left foreground holds a land-mine detector.

The guns of the Utah Beach task force turned the silent, misty French shore between Les Dunes de Varreville and La Madeleine into a churning chaos of dust and smoke and splintered rock. Admiral Deyo's order to advance the firing time had set in motion the seaborne invasion of Europe.

Heavy guns from the *Nevada*, the *Black Prince*, and the monitor *Erebus* threw their full firepower at German batteries above the landing area. Other craft, particularly the destroyers closer to shore, slammed shells into the beach front itself.

Troopships had begun loading American GIs into landing craft hours before. It was a slippery, uncertain business in the darkness and the rough Channel waters. Men and equipment clattered into the small, rocking boats which, once loaded, chugged in wearying circles waiting for H-Hour.

At 4:45 A.M. the landing craft turned their last lap and headed toward the shooting war. As the boats drew closer to land, the GIs crowded shoulder to shoulder could hear the steady, heavy clump of naval guns and the answering fire of German batteries. Through the breaking dawn they made out the big warships pounding the shore, and the 120-odd landing craft of the invasion vanguard.

The first wave was made up of landing craft carrying amphibious tanks; after them came a variety of assault boats bearing infantry and engineer troops. These were mostly the LCVP type, boxlike metal shells about forty-five feet long and fourteen feet wide, designed for efficiency rather than comfort.

The standard LCVP carried an attack team of thirty-two men standing — seats were one of the luxuries eliminated— usually composed of riflemen, BAR (Browning Automatic Rifle) men, specialists in wire cutting and demolition, two bazooka men with assistants to carry extra rockets, flamethrower operators, and medics.

Two patrol craft led the column, along with a radar boat to spy out the shore through the dim light and smoke. There should have been two radar boats, one for each half of the beach area. But one of them had been put out of service by a humiliating accident— a rope had fouled the propeller.

The shore ahead loomed strange. Officers squinted hopefully, trying to discover the landmarks they had been briefed to expect. All that a man could see from the landing craft was an occasional glimpse of a beach that could have been anywhere— obscured, revealed, and then hidden again by flying debris and drifting smoke.

At the very last moment before the Utah landing, the skies disgorged 276 Marauder medium bombers of the U. S. Air Force. They pounded the beach defenses with 550 tons of bombs before the dust had had a chance to settle from the half-hour naval bombardment. When a solitary German fighter plane made a brave pass at the approaching line of landing craft, a British Spitfire plummeted from above

to blow it apart before its threat had registered on the men in the LCVPs.

Then the first wave of invaders hit the beach.

The amphibious tanks (called DDs for the "dual-drive" hook-up by which the tank engine turned two propellers in the water and the regular tracks on land) were especially designed to move quickly from surf to beach and provide supporting fire for the infantry and engineers. They had worked well in the invasion rehearsals, but they were not made for the rough waters off the Normandy beaches.

Canvas inner tubes, called bloomers, had been attached to help float the tanks ashore, but from the first launchings they proved insufficient. Many of the tanks simply disappeared beneath the waves. Only twelve DDs out of the first wave reached the shore to lay down a covering fire.

One LCT dropped its ramp directly on an unswept sea mine, and the explosion blew the lead tank a hundred feet high; it fell back into the sea an armored coffin. LCIs and LCAs developed leaks, and the infantrymen bailed water and cursed. A newspaper correspondent with the first wave heard one wet and seasick GI snarl, "That guy Higgins ain't got nothing to be proud of about inventing this damn boat."

American B-26 Marauders pull up after blasting German coastal defenses in the Utah sector. The low-flying medium bombers operated more effectively in the overcast skies on D-Day than high-altitude heavy bombers.

66

But the first wave was almost precisely on time. At H-Hour the ramps flopped down, and six hundred men surged into waist-deep water to wade the last hundred yards to French soil.

The scheduled landing area was a 2,200-yard stretch just south of Les Dunes de Varreville, easily identified by the large windmill behind the beach. But the men of this first wave, including Brigadier General Theodore Roosevelt, Jr. (a son of the former President), could find neither the expected windmill nor any other landmarks.

What had happened was that the combination of wind, tidal drift, lack of necessary control craft, and the battle smoke that obscured the shore had landed the first troops about a mile farther south than planned. It was an error that added to the morning's confusion, but it was a fortunate error. German defenses were much stronger in the original Utah target area. The new point of assault was comparatively undefended.

The few hundred Germans in dugouts and bunkers behind the beach were still stunned by the firepower that had been poured on them from sea and air. The parachute landings in the Ste. Mère-Eglise area had cut off almost all communication between them and the German reserve forces inland. Their artillery had been partially knocked out by Allied parachute attacks and by bombardment. There was not enough of the Luftwaffe active in the whole area to provide them even token help from the sky.

Now they were faced with a swarming horde from the sea. It was impossible for them to estimate the attackers' numbers in the swirling dust of the continuing barrages, now followed by fire from the DD tanks operating on the beach. The German soldier was superbly trained to combat the predictable, but there had never before in history been anything quite like this. A handful tried to keep up a fire against the invaders; the majority either surrendered or fled to the rear, right into the guns of the parachutists.

There were pile-ups and sinkings to delay the invaders, but still they came, wading heavy with equipment through the waves onto the strange beach.

General Roosevelt, who had insisted on being in the first wave, figured out the mistake in position soon after he hit the beach. The decision facing him now was whether to route the remaining waves to the original target, or to consolidate the new position for the whole Utah operation.

After a quick reconnaissance to check exit routes inland, and encouraged by the lack of enemy resistance, General Roosevelt made the snap judgment to hang on where he was. GIs of the first wave anchored big colored markers in the sand to guide other landing craft toward the new location.

Utah Beach, assigned to the U.S. VII Corps, lay at the base of the Cotentin Peninsula. It was hoped that the troops, who hit the beach a mile south of their assault target (far right), could advance on D-Day as far as the heavy line; the shaded area shows their actual penetration. In the inset picture, GIs move inland past the Utah sea wall.

UTAH BEACH

Montebourg

Fort St. Marcouf

Fontenay-sur-Mer

St. Marcouf

Merderet R.

Foucarville

Les Dunes de Varreville

St. Germain-de-Varreville

St. Martin-de-Varreville

La Madeleine

PROPOSED
LANDING
AREA

ACTUAL
LANDING
AREA

Ste. Mère-Eglise

l'Abbé

Pouppeville

Ste. Marie-du-Mont

Douve R.

Vierville

N

Carentan

Vire R.

0   1   2
MILES

Combat engineers and a group of tank bulldozers hit the beach in the second wave and went to work at once on the obstacles set up by the German defenders. Navy underwater demolition men blew up the first row of barriers at the water's edge as the engineers almost simultaneously blasted the next row.

New waves of landing craft were already crowding dangerously as they headed for the first openings, and the engineer teams hurried to clear the whole beach front for landings. One engineer landing craft sank before reaching the shore, but with minor casualties. The clearing operation went smoothly and effectively. Tank bulldozers uprooted and pushed away what obstacles they could; the engineers blew up the rest.

German "beetles," tiny toy-size tanks carrying explosive charges and designed to be maneuvered and exploded by remote control, failed to function. They were an object of curiosity to the GIs rather than a lethal threat. Within an hour after the landing of the second wave, Utah Beach was clear, and new waves were landing.

Heavy bombardment from the ships offshore continued to help the beach forces. Aerial reconnaissance spotted German strong points and relayed precise information back to the fleet. One German shore battery at Fort St. Marcouf mounted three 210-millimeter guns heavily protected by concrete casemates. From the opening barrage, this battery was a target for Allied ships. One gun was silenced as the landings began, a second took a direct hit from a 15-inch shell fired by the monitor *Erebus* early in the afternoon, and by evening the third and last gun had been destroyed from the sea.

Some German artillery fire from well behind the beach had begun to hit the invaders, but Utah was still a landing comfortably beyond all expectations. Infantry groups and engineer units moved beyond the beach and into its side boundaries to mop up the remaining German troops and strengthen their foothold on enemy soil. Gaps were blown in a sea wall, and the first probing arrows were pointed inland.

Tanks and bulldozers scraped roadways toward the main exit routes across the flooded marshes. German guns zeroed in on the most obvious exit at the southern end of the beach, but the bulldozers just changed direction and cut new lanes out of the fire area.

The helmsman of an assault craft in one of the later landing waves, amazingly ignorant of the fact that the target area had been changed, determinedly steered his craft to the original spot, now a deserted stretch of peaceful sand. Bewildered, he changed course just offshore and brought his passengers a mile south, where they could see a war going on. Not until they landed did they learn that they had sailed right past the guns of an uncaptured German battery. The quick success of the first landings had taken the heart out of Hitler's defenders at Utah.

With only minor opposition, men of

the 8th Infantry Regiment mopped up the German fortifications in and around La Madeleine, about half a mile inland from the northern tip of Utah. Other units of the 8th cleared houses and all likely hiding places along the beach and beside. the exit routes north and south of La Madeleine. Continuing waves landed on the beach, were organized, and joined the advance inland.

A rough but effective order came into being on the sands that a few hours before had not even figured in the invasion plans. Supplies were stacked up under tarpaulins. Radios chattered from command posts, reporting progress back to the headquarters ships offshore, relaying new orders to advance units, and slowly sorting out the whole pattern of the landing that was breaching the walls of Fortress Europe.

Such communication was spotty—many radios had been lost and others were damaged in the landing—but it was sufficient to let Major General J. Lawton Collins, VII Corps commander in charge of Utah, know that things were going well. The scarcity and confusion of communications forced General Collins to stay aboard the attack transport *Bayfield* or lose touch completely with Lieutenant General Omar Bradley aboard the heavy cruiser *Augusta*, off Omaha Beach.

Collins also had to keep in close touch with the naval support force. At one point in the afternoon, an admiral was ready to suspend landing operations temporarily, due to ship losses,

and it was only General Collins' quick intervention that kept the invasion waves rolling on to Utah.

German reaction was slow, hampered by delay and confusion, crippled by lack of air support, and most of all, frozen in a stubborn misconception. Although the fact of invasion was clear from dawn onward, German Intelligence was reluctant to believe that what was happening was *the* invasion.

The whole German strategy had been pegged on repelling an attack on the Pas-de-Calais. They continued to hold back their forces in readiness for

A Navy beach party examines German "beetles" abandoned at Utah. These small tanks, holding a hundred pounds of explosives, were aimed at Allied armor by remote control.
NATIONAL ARCHIVES

OVERLEAF: *This grim scene was painted by an American combat artist. Medics remove casualties from a half-track, coming ashore on D-Day, that was riddled by German fire.*
COMBAT ART SECTION, U.S. NAVY

such an attack, and against continuing evidence from the beaches, lulled themselves into a belief that the shore defense garrisons could throw back or at least contain the threat of June 6.

Hitler's headquarters got word of the Allied airborne landings before the beaches had been hit, but dismissed them as feints. Not until late in the morning of June 6 were the assaults recognized as even part of a full-scale invasion. Communication to and from Germany was uncertain. The news of the Utah landings did not penetrate to the Fuehrer's command post until afternoon.

Field Marshal Rommel had received the news earlier. At 10:30 A.M. his chief of staff, Major General Hans Speidel, called his home at Herrlingen in Germany, far from the battle front. Rommel heard the whole of Speidel's report before responding. When he spoke it was only to say, "How stupid of me. How stupid of me." Putting down the phone he called his aide to get transportation to Normandy as quickly as possible.

The German Fifteenth Army was stolidly planted in the Somme area north of Paris; only a few of its armored divisions had been transferred at the last moment to Normandy where they could do some good.

The death of a German Junkers 88 bomber, strafed at point-blank range by a hedge-hopping American fighter, was recorded by the fighter's automatic camera. Such attacks had crippled the Luftwaffe by D-Day.

The German Seventh Army was responsible for Normandy, but its effective striking forces were concentrated far back, a good one hundred miles southeast of the landing points. Two armored divisions were finally ordered into the invasion area. However, because of the destruction of traffic arteries by Allied bombers, they advanced at a snail's pace.

As for the German Air Force, it was hardly to be seen. There had been talk in German command circles earlier in the year of massing air power along the French coast to repel a possible assault, but Reichsmarshal Hermann Goering made the final decision against the move. To expose his valuable and dwindling stock of fighter and attack planes on fields so close to Allied raiders seemed to him to be inviting destruction.

Also, to remove fighter squadrons from Germany, already reeling under Allied air raids, would have been a dangerous blow to civilian morale. The raids were bad enough without forcing the population to forego the sight of occasional Messerschmitts aloft to knock down a few of the bombers. So D-Day saw the French coast stripped of sufficient German planes to attack the troops packed tightly on the beaches, or to make even a dent in the covering swarm of Allied bombers and fighters. During the daylight hours of June 6, the Luftwaffe delivered but 250 sorties against the invasion forces.

Even as late waves of engineers and quartermaster troops were turning Utah into a permanent beachhead, the German high command clung to its estimate that it would take the Allies up to a week to land five or six divisions. The estimate made no allowance for the incredible number of British and American troops pouring across the Channel, or for the newly-devised artificial harbor facilities.

The sea invaders were soon making contact with the airborne forces. Moving through the southernmost beach exit, a detachment of 4th Division GIs had knocked out a German pillbox with the help of an amphibious tank and was headed for a small bridge on the road to Pouppeville. They saw a few Germans run toward them and then dive for cover beneath the bridge. The Americans advanced cautiously to capture the Germans and heard sounds of firing from Pouppeville. They hoisted their orange signal flag and, minutes later, were shaking hands and slapping backs with men of the 101st Airborne.

By early afternoon Utah Beach had absorbed almost a full division, and by nightfall even the most conservative military pessimist would have had to admit that the Utah operation was a sensational success.

The beach itself was by then a well-organized landing area, swept clean of land mines and obstacles and functioning smoothly. Some advance parties had established strong points as much as six miles beyond the beach, well past the flooded marshes and in control of key roadways. There were still some

American troops, dug in on the Normandy shore, watch U.S. heavy bombers streaming back to England. Barrage balloons float over the beach to hamper Luftwaffe strafing planes.

76

well-armed pockets of German resistance here and there, but the Americans held a vital oval-shaped beachhead extending just beyond Ste. Mère-Eglise and stretching from St. Germain-de-Varreville to the Vire River.

Three main arteries were open and in use from the beach. Almost all major objectives had been achieved, and the cost was amazingly low. Out of the thousands of men engaged in the landing, only twelve were killed and about one hundred wounded. There were more casualties from landing craft accidents than from enemy fire.

In his mountain retreat, Adolf Hitler failed to absorb the significance of what was happening. The order transmitted to his Seventh Army radiated an optimism that could not have been shared by German troops at Utah: "Chief of Staff Western Command emphasizes the desire of the Supreme Command to have the enemy in the bridgehead annihilated by the evening of June 6 since there exists the danger of additional sea- and airborne landings for support. . . the beachhead must be cleaned up by not later than tonight."

At the time the message was sent, there was no German defense to speak of at the Utah beachhead. It was a firmly established American position, constantly replenished by new landings, sending its probing forces inland as the night fell. Utah Beach was a piece of good luck in a massive invasion that just now, only a few miles away, needed all the luck it could get.

5.

Bloody Omaha

The story of Omaha Beach stands in stark contrast to what happened at Utah.

In the predawn hours, mine sweepers and buoy ships marked paths all the way to the beach without incident. Troopships and warships, led by the majestic *Arkansas*, the oldest battleship in the United States Navy, took up their positions. The infantry landing craft began to load up for the long and seasick circling before H-Hour.

The loading area, eleven miles offshore to keep out of range of the German coastal battery at Pointe du Hoc, gave the first hint of troubles to come. Strong winds and high waves created conditions even more dangerous than the choppy waters off Utah.

At 5:30 A.M. the *Arkansas* opened up the prelanding bombardment of shore targets. Two French cruisers joined in the punishing barrage that was a necessary start to the liberation of their homeland. The battleship *Texas* trained her 14-inch guns on Pointe du Hoc, which Allied Intelligence had listed as "the most dangerous battery in France." The ships furnished the same merciless bombardment that had been laid on Utah. There was only light return fire from the shore. So far, so good.

Lanes for the landing craft were clearly marked, and there would be no repetition of the Utah drift away from the general target area. Omaha was a wider beach than Utah, extending eastward some 6,000 yards from Vierville almost to Le Grand Hameau. The planners had divided it into seven separate assault sectors.

Omaha did not offer the flat terrain of Utah. It was backed by bluffs and sheer cliffs up to 170 feet high, forming a long, concave target with the highest cliffs at either end. The beach was firm sand for about three hundred yards, but then it rose swiftly and steeply in stony banks. The western end had, in addition to this natural barrier, a heavy sea wall with more steep banks behind it.

Cutting through the high bluffs were four main outlets, which led to towns and road centers behind the beach area. The strategic value of these exits was as apparent to the Germans as it was to the attacking Americans, and unlike Utah, Omaha was defended by first-class troops, dug in and determined.

Navy artist Dwight Shepler painted this troop-carrying LCI, straddled by German mortar shells, aground among the beach obstacles at Omaha. Soldiers trapped on board seek cover from the vicious fire.

In this section, Rommel had been able to install his most extensive anti-invasion defenses. Along the water line were three rows of solidly planted obstacles, steel-and-concrete pilings slanting seaward to snag invading craft. Some of the pilings were equipped with mines.

The beach itself was thickly sown with mines and covered with tangles of barbed wire. Guns in concrete emplacements commanded the whole sandy expanse, most also sited to control the exits that led inland. On top of the cliffs at either end of the area were especially strong batteries. Carefully concealed and protected by tons of reinforced concrete, they were able to resist the toughest battering from the naval guns offshore. There were other defenses all along the beach between these strong points, none of them quite so impregnable, but all of them capable of giving an invading force a very ugly reception.

Omaha resembled nothing so much as a giant trap. Yet there was no other spot along the coast where major landings would have been possible. The shore on either side presented cliffs rising sheer from the water; at least at Omaha there was some beach.

As the moment of landing drew closer, loading difficulties multiplied into disorder and death. DD tanks, as at Utah, failed to live up to their amphibious promise. Thirty-six of them were scheduled to land ahead of the first infantry wave to furnish fire-power and support for the eastern

beaches. Unloaded in choppy seas 5,000 yards from shore, their canvas bloomers collapsed, and tank after tank sank to the bottom; survivors in life belts bobbed to the surface, only to be killed by German fire.

Most of the tanks that did not go down immediately foundered before they reached the shore. Only five of the thirty-six tanks reached the beach and went into action, and three of these made it because the naval officer in charge of an LCT, after losing one tank in offshore launching, insisted on running his craft right up to the beach.

Things were a little better in the western section, where twenty-eight DD tanks and fourteen standard tanks made the beach. German defensive fire took a heavy toll, but the remainder were able to offer support for the following infantry.

One of the most important requirements for a successful landing at Omaha, according to the best Allied information, was to knock out the powerful six-gun German battery at Pointe du Hoc. These 155-millimeter guns, in concrete casemates atop a sheer 117-foot cliff, commanded the whole beach area. It seemed to be an impossible stronghold, and one Allied officer, briefed on the plan to capture it, snapped, "Three old women with

The four natural exits through the bluffs behind Omaha Beach can be seen on this map. The shaded area is the American beachhead at the end of D-Day, far short of the intended goal indicated by the heavy line. The Rangers in the picture herd prisoners down the steep cliffs. Ranger units attacked the Pointe du Hoc battery (upper left).

Hoc

OMAHA BEACH

Pointe et Raz
de la Percée

N

Vierville

Les Moulins

Vacqueville

St. Laurent

Montigny

Le Grand Hameau

Longueville

Colleville

Formigny

Surain

Bellefontaine

Aure R.

Trévières

mbières

Bricqueville

Blay

0   1   2

MILES

La Commune

Vaubadon

brooms could keep the Rangers from climbing that cliff!''

But the cliff had to be climbed, and the job was handed to two hundred men of the United States 2nd Ranger Battalion. Naval support from the destroyers U.S.S. *Satterlee* and H.M.S. *Talybont* held down enemy fire while the Rangers made their approach in amphibious trucks. As the Rangers scaled the cliff, the plainly visible German defenders were sprayed with fire from the supporting naval craft. Extension ladders borrowed from the London Fire Brigade swayed from the trucks, with Rangers on the top rungs peppering the cliff top with BARs and submachine guns.

Some 150 Rangers clambered up the cliff face and reached the battery. The defenders had rifles and grenades instead of brooms, but they were no match for the determined assault team.

When the Rangers examined their prize, they found six wooden telephone poles. The actual guns, because of which the Allied launching operation had been carried out so perilously in the wild waters eleven miles from shore, had been spirited away to be refitted with new defensive armor. Nothing was left but the hollow concrete fortress, manned by garrison troops who were hunted down by the Rangers. (Later, a Ranger patrol advancing inland found four of the missing guns, camouflaged and in a position to pour fire onto Utah Beach. They wrecked them with grenades, accomplishing their objective after all.)

Somehow, in these crucial moments, the Pointe du Hoc Rangers lost radio communication with seaborne headquarters. Troops standing by to reinforce the strike were held back. It was assumed that the assault had failed, and the Ranger reinforcements were sent elsewhere.

Omaha was to have had the same sort of last-minute aerial bombardment as Utah, but a cloudy overcast hampered the plan. To avoid bombing the landing craft nearing the shore, the heavy bombers were told to delay their bomb drop for thirty seconds. The infantrymen cheered when they heard the B-24s thunder overhead, but most of them were bewildered when the bombs dropped uselessly far beyond the German beach defenses. Naval bombardment continued to be virtually the only support the GIs could count on.

There were continuing disasters in loading and launching the assault. Not only the DD tanks were victims. Fifteen landing craft packed with troops were swamped by waves and sank with all aboard. German defensive fire spattered over the beaches and the surf the moment the naval guns providing the preinvasion barrage fell silent.

The famous combat photographer Robert Capa took this picture of an American infantryman bound for the Omaha holocaust.

OVERLEAF: *H-Hour at Omaha—ominous, smoke-wreathed bluffs loom in the background as the first invaders hit the beach.*

Despite the best efforts of mine sweepers, a few German sea mines drifted into the assault channels. These men were rescued from an LCVP blown apart by one of them.

"You couldn't talk about which wave was which," remembers Lieutenant John F. Schereschewsky, a onetime Harvard fullback in command of a landing craft on D-Day. "Assault waves piled back into each other. What I recall most is the yellowish-gray smoke that shrouded the whole shore. That, and not being able to see any of the guns firing on us. The Germans had their guns placed to enfilade [flank] the beaches, and it wasn't until you looked to either side that you caught flashes of orange fire in the ugly smoke."

Schereschewsky had spent seven solid hours reading the sheaf of orders for his route and going over invasion charts. These showed the positions of all known German batteries, and the lieutenant found them too depressing to take along. He put them to one side and plotted his course on a British Admiralty map that had all the pertinent information, but did not emphasize that boats were to beach into enormous enemy firepower.

When he took his LCI into the assigned zone, all hell seemed loose there. He found not only enemy fire, but huge, scooped-out craters in the offshore sand as much as fifty yards across, the result of the battleship shelling. At first Schereschewsky thought the beach was covered with driftwood. Then he realized that what he saw were bodies.

The LCI ahead of him touched shore, and he saw GIs rush down its ramp into the surf; suddenly, where their heads had been, he saw only their feet. The LCI was perched on the edge of a deep crater, and the infantrymen, loaded with heavy equipment and with their life belts too low on their bodies, had been turned over in the deep surf. Schereschewsky ordered full speed astern and pulled out, with mortar and artillery shells splashing the water around him.

With the two surviving LCIs of his unit, he moved westward to the beach sector labeled Easy Red. The fire here was still heavy, but there were no craters. The worst difficulty was jammed traffic. Dodging between LCIs and LCTs, Schereschewsky brought his craft to shore, only to hear from his group commander, aboard another boat, the voice of official planning: "What are you doing here? You're supposed to be at Fox Green!" The lieutenant shouted back a suitable retort. He had saved a boatload of infantrymen from drowning, and group commanders could holler until they were hoarse.

The thirty-five minutes of heavy fire from the ships had hit many of its objectives and had driven the German defenders under cover, but it had not yet been able to make a really crippling impression on the heavy concrete bastions on the bluffs and cliffs commanding the beach. Not only were these positions stronger and more numerous than at Utah, but they were manned by crack, battle-hardened German troops of the 352nd Division.

This superior combat division had been quietly transferred into the Omaha Beach area three months before D-Day, and its presence there was completely unknown to Allied Intelligence. The men of the 352nd sat out the naval barrage with professional patience and, once it was over, calmly trained their weapons on the beach.

Here there was no triumphant drive inland as at Utah. GIs landed in a withering fire. Those who survived were lucky to find and hold a protected position on the beach; there was little chance to move forward. Although the over-all landing was made closer to the planned area than at Utah, there were vastly greater mix-ups among individual units. On a more condensed scale, it was much the same story as the confusion of the paratroop drops during the night.

Because of the tidal drift, units destined for one part of the beach wound up in another. The first wave for the Easy Red sector was bunched into one corner of its target area; other units lost their officers and huddled in planless bewilderment. Attempts to organize were blown to bits by the savagery of the German defense. Simply to survive was an accomplishment.

The casualties and confusions of the first wave affected every succeeding wave. LCVPs landed their troops fifty or a hundred yards offshore, and GIs waded into enemy fire neck-deep in bloody water, achingly holding their rifles above their heads as they stumbled blindly toward the beach. Once ashore they sought any sort of cover, however shallow and temporary, behind which they could dig in and fire back. Men advanced as in a nightmare, watching their friends pitch grotesquely into the water or fall on the beach to add new stains to the sand.

Engineer and naval demolition teams had no chance to function properly. Launching delays prevented half the engineers from hitting the beach at their appointed time, and when they did land, only a third came close to their objectives. The rest were carried away by the tide and then pinned in their useless positions by enemy fire. Much of their equipment was lost in the heavy seas, and those units in their proper spots were unable to breach the sea wall or clear obstacles.

Only three armored bulldozers out of sixteen were able to operate at all on the beach. Of these three, at least one was hampered in its clearing job, not by German fire, but by American infantrymen; cheated of any natural cover, they clustered in the shelter of the big machine and protested any movement. Less than an hour after the first landings, the tide rose and covered the German shore obstacles so that no more clearing was possible for hours.

The only fire support Omaha could count on was from the Navy. Destroyers, so close to shore that some of them almost ran aground, kept up steady fire against German batteries. U.S.S. *McCook* whaled away at enemy guns on the cliff near Pointe et Râz de la Percée and was rewarded when one emplacement blew up and another fell right off the side of the cliff onto the beach. There was almost no effective shore-to-ship radio communication for spotting objectives, and the destroyers fired as best they could at "targets of opportunity." *McCook* had thrown 975 rounds into the beach by evening.

Salvos from battleships, fired at greater range, could not be so precisely centered on the beaches as destroyer fire, but they pummeled German targets farther inland and discouraged the movement of troops. British Spitfires searched out enemy positions from the air and radioed their exact locations to U.S.S. *Texas*. Thus, the *Texas* smashed German units as far as three miles inland.

The whole width of Omaha Beach presented a bloody and chaotic scene. Yet some of the invaders still managed to perform miracles of endurance and heroism. The engineers suffered casualties of some sixty per cent during the morning, but they kept trying to blow

Over half the engineers in the first waves were hit trying to clear Omaha of landing-craft obstacles. This crew plants a demolition charge as a German shell splashes nearby.

up the obstacles before the tide denied them their targets. One enlisted man in a tank bulldozer uprooted German obstacles until enemy fire wrecked it; then he sprinted across the shot-torn sand, already thick with casualties, to another bulldozer and continued his work.

The later waves came in to face the same relentless fire. The sector near Vierville continued to be the zone of the worst confusion. Landing craft were sunk by German batteries, and machine guns raked the open beach below the cliff as survivors struggled to find some safety behind the sea wall.

Here the leading units of the 116th Infantry Regiment were almost completely wiped out. Of its 1st Battalion only one company survived to operate as an organized unit. The sand and the concrete sea wall were rusty red with bloodstains. It took the heavy-weapons company of the 2nd Battalion two hours just to assemble its survivors and to save, from all its equipment, a total of three mortars, three machine guns, and a small pile of usable ammunition.

The same tragic story unfolded

eastward on the beach. A handful of tanks did their best to reply to German fire, but most of the enemy emplacements were out of reach on the heights above the shore. The dead and dying littered the sand, and medics darted out from the cover of the sea wall to try to give first aid or to tug a wounded comrade to shelter.

A medic found a wounded soldier sitting calmly on the beach with one leg slashed open from knee to hip so deeply that the medic could see the femoral artery pulsing; he gave the casualty a shot of morphine and did the best he could to close the wound by using safety pins. It was not the place for delicate surgical techniques.

Marking and signal equipment had been scattered or lost, and new waves aimed at their assigned sectors as best they could. Among the first casualties had been a high proportion of company commanders and platoon leaders. Groups of men sought shelter where they found it, with no one to direct them. Some GIs cried from fear, from sheer frustration, or from a mix-

To take this picture, Robert Capa braved the same savage fire that forced infantrymen to seek the cover of beach obstacles or to crouch behind amphibious tanks crawling ashore.

ture of the two. When men did try to move, the uncleared land back of the beach was a deadly hazard. There was no telling when a concealed mine might blow a running soldier to shreds.

The lack of firepower to take care of German pillboxes continued to plague the Omaha landings. While naval support helped, the real need was for artillery support on the beach itself, and desperate measures were tried. A batch of 37-millimeter antiaircraft guns, mounted on half-tracks, arrived in one sector; since German planes were no problem, they were pressed into service to help the troops pinned to the beach. One of them, parked in the surf with water lapping into its cab, drew a bead on a particularly offensive German pillbox on the bluffs and knocked it out with ten rounds.

Naval shelling of German positions

The German 88-millimeter gun above, flanking Omaha Beach, was wrecked by naval gunfire. Heavily protected by concrete, particularly on the seaward side, it usually took a direct hit to knock out such emplacements.

Conditions on Omaha were still grim by midafternoon of D-Day (right). Troops and medics were dug in behind the sea wall as German shelling continued; the wounded awaiting evacuation lay exposed on the beach.

continued, but many of the concrete casemates held out against anything but a direct hit. To the German officers it seemed that Omaha was proving the impregnability of Field Marshal Rommel's defense measures.

From his protected post at Pointe et Raz de la Percée, the local German commandant had a sweeping view of an invasion seemingly stopped cold. He saw swamped landing craft and wrecked tanks and bulldozers, helpless clusters of men pinned to the base of the sea wall, and hundreds of ant-size dots signifying the bodies of GIs foolish enough to believe that Hitler's

Atlantic Wall might be vulnerable. The officer sent back a proud and optimistic report to von Rundstedt: "The American invasion is stopped on the beaches. Heavy losses are being inflicted on the survivors. The beaches are littered with burning vehicles and dead and dying troops. Heil Hitler."

As far as Allied leaders were concerned—particularly General Omar Bradley, anxiously trying to make sense out of the scrambled battle reports in his headquarters on the cruiser *Augusta*—the German commandant might have been right. Radio communication was garbled and de-

pressing. One division had only a quarter of its radios working; the remaining seventy-five per cent had been lost or made useless by sea water, sand, or enemy fire.

Writing later, General Bradley admitted that the battle "had run beyond the reach of its admirals and generals." According to the best information he had at noon, the situation at Omaha was a seesaw affair, with victory as likely to tilt to one side as the other.

In this grim hour he had to face the possibility of writing off Omaha entirely, leaving the troops clinging to the narrow beach to their fate, and sending his remaining forces to Utah or to the British beaches. It was at 1:30, seven hours after the first troops had landed, that the radio aboard the *Augusta* sounded a thin note of hope: "Troops formerly pinned down . . . advancing up heights behind beaches."

The battle that had swirled out of the hands of the admirals and generals was being saved from disaster by the dogged refusal of the troops on the beach to give up.

Another important factor was the limited, fixed quality of the German defense. Good as it was, it was static. Once a German pillbox was knocked

out, once a German gun was silenced, there was nothing to replace it. Despite Rommel's urging, few reserves of men and armor had been stationed behind the coast to launch a counterattack.

The Americans, battered and broken as they were, kept on coming. Wave after wave poured ashore, and gradually, as the day moved into late afternoon, the balance of power along the beach began to shift by just the hair's breadth needed to spell the difference between victory and defeat.

Leaderless men created their own leaders or were inspired to action by those officers left to command. A sergeant here, a private there, became more disgusted with doing nothing than with the threat of death and rallied a platoon or a company to move up the bluffs against German strong points.

Brigadier General Norman Cota stamped up and down the beach, ignoring bullets whining around him and driving troops forward. In the Vierville sector, he found a group of men sheltered near a bulldozer loaded with TNT, just what was needed to blow up the wall that blocked the exit inland. "Hasn't anyone got guts enough to drive the damn thing?" he taunted them. He got his volunteer and then turned his back and headed down the beach to stir up more men.

Aboard the cruiser Augusta, *Rear Admiral Alan G. Kirk (left), commanding the American naval forces, and Lt. General Omar N. Bradley (second from left), head of the U.S. 1st Army, grimly watch the Omaha landings.*

At some points the fighting was on the most personal level. A GI would throw a single grenade, silencing a German machine gun that had been holding down a whole company on the beach; or a handful of men would dash into point-blank fire to knock out an enemy emplacement. Colonel Charles Canham of the 116th Regiment expressed this courage born of desperation when he rallied his men with the cry, "They're murdering us here! Let's move inland and get murdered!"

The Rangers who had taken the Pointe du Hoc battery, however, were coming very close to getting murdered inland. Cut off from both paratroopers and beach forces, they were pushed back into a corner by German counterattacks late in the afternoon. Other Ranger units and men of the 116th Infantry tried to rescue them, but the Germans kept the advantage of their higher position on the bluffs and held them off for two days. By the time the Rangers were relieved on June 8, the battalion was down to ninety men.

Little by little, the series of small victories, every one of them savage and bloody, began to make inroads in the German band of steel and concrete. It was decided early that Omaha must have continuing support from naval gunfire, despite the risk that some of the shells might fall short and hit American troops. This policy was proving its wisdom. Some German strong points were knocked out by the bombardment from the sea, and shells pounding into the area behind them

This painting shows vividly the confusion at Omaha. Milling assault craft seek clear lanes to the beach as the destroyer Emmons *(right) moves in to blast German strong points.*

Above, wounded are evacuated in an LCVP; the man at center clutches a hard-won trophy— a German helmet. Below, a GI too badly hurt to move is given blood plasma.

cut off any German reinforcements.

Omaha shared the same good fortune as Utah in having no Luftwaffe opposition. The soldiers of the German 352nd Division reported unhappily that throughout the whole of D-Day they had not seen a single German plane in the air. What German air action there was concentrated on Allied shipping; this was of little consolation to the Germans trying to hold their concrete boxes against an enemy which suddenly refused to admit that his invasion had failed.

As the tide fell, demolition teams, under a less vicious fire than in the morning, were at last able to take care of the obstacles along the water line. Other crews blew holes in the sea wall and cleared mine fields. Despite continuing opposition, there were now eleven boat channels open to the beach, and it was possible to land increasing numbers of troops, tanks, and artillery without the hideous mishaps that had beset the first waves.

The 1st Division veterans of North Africa and Sicily proved the value of their combat experience. Lieutenant Schereschewsky remembers the men he ferried over. "At first I thought I was getting the dregs. They seemed like old men, uninterested and hunched over in the boat. It was only when they moved toward combat that you saw them as troops who really knew their job, competent and hard to panic." One officer watched in horror as a 1st Division sergeant, moving back to the shore after leading a platoon through the German barbed wire, stepped on an exposed land mine. "It didn't go off when I stepped on it going up either, captain," the sergeant explained, and went about rallying more troops.

The American hold on the beach was becoming steadily stronger. While dangerous pockets of German resistance remained along the rear of the beach, the GIs had proved they could be knocked out.

At Vierville the battered 116th Regiment had pried itself loose from the beach. With Ranger reinforcements and the aid of the bulldozer full of TNT shoved into action by General Cota, the regiment had broken through the sea wall and moved inland.

Farther east, bulldozers cleared a roadway to the main exit toward St. Laurent, and Rangers and other elements of the 116th pushed forward past German strong points to blockade the coastal road to enemy reserves.

All along the beach the invaders inched ahead, taking German defenses when they could, bypassing them when they proved too strong. Once the movement had started, it was less important to knock out every German pillbox than to keep the tide of men rolling inland.

By now the Germans were almost as worried about Omaha as they had been earlier about Utah and the British beaches. Their calls for reinforcements remained unanswered. Most of the available reserves were headed toward what German generals felt was the more critical area at Caen, where the

Above, victorious GIs atop a battered German emplacement wave at American Thunderbolt fighter-bombers streaking low over the shore on the evening of June 6. The somber painting at left, by Navy combat artist Mitchell Jamieson, shows German prisoners of war digging graves for the Omaha dead on a hilltop behind the beach.

British landings were taking place. Besides, there simply were not enough reinforcements to go around.

The two strong armored divisions stationed between Normandy and Paris belonged to a reserve force under Hitler's personal control. Von Rundstedt could not order them into action without getting the Fuehrer's approval, and Hitler, elated by the first news from Omaha and still fearful of a second invasion thrust at the Pas-de-Calais, refused to release them. When he did, in late afternoon, it was too late.

At nightfall on June 6, the American V Corps' foothold on Omaha was not a sure thing, but it was a foothold where for the first six or seven hours it had been barely a toehold. Allowing for some spots of German strength still not cleaned up, Americans controlled the area from Vierville east to Le Grand Hameau. Whereas the Utah beachhead stretched five miles inland, the grip on Omaha was little more than 1,500 yards deep. But they were precious yards that the Germans had lost forever.

This narrow strip of French coast labeled Omaha had cost heavily in killed, wounded, and missing, but it had opened up what became a major gateway for the liberation of Europe. It had added a bitter and bright new name to the annals of American military heroism. In one 1st Division battalion alone, 740 men earned Bronze Stars.

No one who was at Omaha Beach on the sixth of June would ever forget it.

Victory at Omaha: a long line of captured German soldiers trudges down the stretch of Normandy beach they fought so ferociously to hold against the American invaders.

British troops aboard a transport were sketched filing into assault craft on D-Day. They had been waiting for this moment since 1940, when the German Army drove them from France.

6.

The British Landings

The British beaches covered the longest stretch of all, and the landings there varied from the comparatively easy success of Utah to the savagery of Omaha.

The three beaches—Gold, Juno, and Sword—ran for some twenty miles, from Port-en-Bessin on the west to the mouth of the Orne River on the east. Gold, at the western end, started at Port-en-Bessin and extended to La Rivière. Juno began at this point and ended at St. Aubin. Sword carried the assault area to the Orne delta, just out of range of the heavy German shore batteries at Le Havre.

This was also the largest strike in manpower. Three divisions were involved: the British 3rd and 50th and the Canadian 3rd, plus units of Free French troops. Their target was the most critically important to the Germans; a breakthrough here would threaten the great port of Le Havre and put the Allies on the high road to Paris itself. The Allies had no doubts that the landings would be fiercely contested.

The Britishers in the first D-Day waves were not the first to set foot on the Normandy beaches in the course of the war. Throughout the winter and early spring, two British commandos, Logan Scott-Bowden and Ogden Smith, had been conducting their own

GOLD

Port-en-Bessin

Aure R.

Arromanches

Le Hamel

La Rivière

Bayeux

Seulles R.

LCL 299

IMPERIAL WAR MUSEUM

private invasions. Nearly every moon-less night they swam ashore from a midget submarine to scout the terrain.

The daring pair was never spotted—although once a German sentry on beach patrol walked right between them and even tripped over their guide line—and the information they brought back was of great value to the invasion planners. For one thing, Scott-Bowden and Smith found the sandy beaches packed hard enough to support tanks and other heavy vehicles.

The British midget submarines X-20 and X-23 arrived at either end of the landing beaches on June 3, carrying

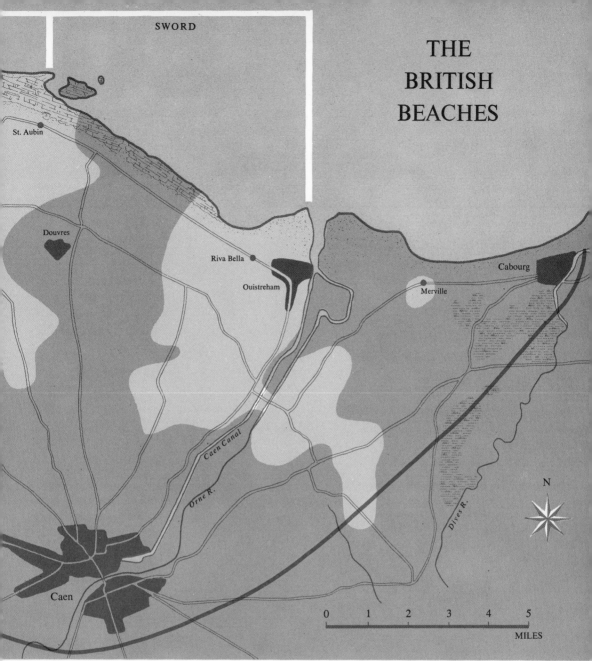

SWORD

THE
BRITISH
BEACHES

St. Aubin

Douvres

Riva Bella

Ouistreham

Merville

Cabourg

Caen Canal

Orne R.

Dives R.

N

Caen

| 0 | 1 | 2 | 3 | 4 | 5 |

MILES

MAP BY MARTHA BLAKE

crews ready to mark the boundaries of the target area. The change in the invasion date to June 6 meant that the subs had to keep submerged for an extra twenty-four hours; at 4:45 on the morning of the sixth they surfaced, and the men went to work. After sixty-four cramped hours under water, even the

The shaded portion of this map shows the British D-Day beachhead. They failed on June 6 to reach the heavy "objective" line and to capture Caen and Bayeux, but the next day they closed the vulnerable gap between Juno and Sword and took Bayeux. The Canadian infantrymen in the picture wade ashore at Juno, some carrying bicycles.

grim prospect of two hours in clear view of enemy shore guns was a relief. They raised masts and put into operation the blinker lights that would guide the invaders.

The Channel crossing to the British beaches was much like that of the other task forces, with one major exception. The ships bound for Sword were the only ones to tangle with the German Navy on D-Day.

Admiral Krancke's headquarters had been roused to action by reports of the paratroop jumps in the early morning, and he belatedly ordered his torpedo boats out to patrol the Channel. At 5:30 A.M. three of them blundered through the smoke screen laid by Allied planes to hide the armada from the batteries at Le Havre. Their routine patrol had led them smack into the middle of the landing force. Jumping at their unexpected advantage, they loosed eighteen torpedoes into the fleet, turned back into the protective smoke screen, and raced for safety.

The results should have been like shooting fish in a barrel, but luck was with the British. Two torpedoes passed between the battleships *Warspite* and *Ramillies*, and all the rest save one wobbled around and between other ships without inflicting any damage.

An English soldier painted these water colors of the Juno landing. At the top, a tank burns furiously as infantrymen pick their cautious way through beach obstacles. Below, tanks landed from a pair of beached LCTs drive past a smoldering German gun emplacement.

The eighteenth torpedo found the Norwegian destroyer *Svenner*. It was a solid strike amidships, and the *Svenner* broke in two and sank with a loss of thirty-four lives.

Tide conditions in the British area called for a later landing hour than at the two American beaches, and the Royal Navy made good use of the extra time. It bombarded the shore for close to two hours, four times longer than the barrages at Utah and Omaha, making up for the fact that Gold, Juno, and Sword had no prelanding aerial strikes.

At 7:25 A.M. landing craft began to hit the shore. Frogmen swam in first to blow up beach obstacles, but the invasion force was so close on their heels that there were immediate pile-ups of landing craft along the shore.

In these first waves were commando units of five hundred men apiece, especially picked and trained, with each unit containing Free French soldiers to deal with French civilians on shore. The British sector was much more thickly populated than either Utah or Omaha, and the Free French commandos were to pacify citizens who might be more indignant over the bombardment than grateful for liberation. Some of these units scorned the steel helmets of regular troops and proudly wore green berets into combat.

Gold Beach, except for its westernmost sector, was not too difficult once the initial tie-up at the beach obstacles had been straightened out. The enemy defenders were mostly troops of the

Commandos lie on the shore under fire, waiting for orders to move inland. The Germans had made strong points out of the beach villas, like those in the background, that dotted the British landing area.

German 716th Division, a mixture of Polish and Ukrainian "volunteers" whose patriotic devotion to Hitler was slight. Some British units advanced jauntily, singing army songs.

Lieutenant Alan Houghton of the Royal Navy beached his LCI and saw its combat team move off into a quiet landscape barren of enemy fire. It was so calm and pleasant that Houghton and two of his officers decided to take a short sight-seeing stroll before returning to England.

Chatting amiably, they walked across the beach to a French farmhouse bordering the sand. They went in through the open door and explored the deserted rooms on the first floor. Suddenly they heard footsteps on the floor above, conversation in German, and a burst of firing. The lieutenant and his friends were standing underneath a fifteen-man German snipers' nest.

The three Navy men had but one pistol among them. One crept out, found some infantrymen who provided him with rifles, and slipped back inside. The naval task force was now in a good position. They could spot the Germans above them from their footsteps and fire up through the ceiling; the Germans could not guess where to aim at their unexpected assailants. There was a short exchange of fire which killed one of the snipers and wounded another. Then the Germans surrendered. Lieutenant Houghton turned them over to combat troops and returned to his LCI after a most satisfying and rewarding stroll.

At the western end of Gold the invaders hit a tougher foe, the capable and well-entrenched troops of the 352nd Division whose comrades were pinning down the Americans at Omaha.

Mortar and machine-gun fire raked the beach, cutting down man after man of the 1st Hampshire Regiment as they waded ashore. The Hampshires kept moving ahead doggedly toward the enemy strong points, but it would be midafternoon before they silenced the German guns in and around Le Hamel and were able to move inland. They left two hundred dead and wounded behind them.

The British had a unique array of weapons to help speed their beach advances. Their engineers and designers had made a careful study of the lessons taught by the ill-fated commando raid on the French Channel port of Dieppe in August of 1942, lessons that the Americans at Omaha were learning the hard way.

Dieppe had proved to the British that engineer troops held down by enemy fire were in no condition to carry out their missions of clearing mine fields or blowing up obstacles. To help the engineers, British inventors had devised a whole new series of tanks lumped together under the name "funnies." The DD tank, which had proved a death trap in rough water, was the only one of the funnies that the American forces had adopted. Other truly valuable types had been scorned or ignored.

These bore such odd-sounding

The moment an assault area was secured and cleared it was turned into a supply port. In this panoramic view of Gold Beach, landing craft crowd ashore to unload men and tanks.

names as flails, bobbins and roly-polys, fascines, self-propelled ramps, bridging tanks, petards, and crocodiles.

Flail tanks had revolving drums mounted in front from which a number of chains and rods lashed the ground and blew up land mines with no harm to anything but eardrums. Bobbins and roly-polys unrolled carpets of steel mesh or heavy matting to form a temporary road. Fascines hauled great bundles of logs that could be dropped into antitank ditches to make them passable. The thirty-foot spans carried by the bridging tanks were to be laid across streams or bomb craters.

Self-propelled ramps were smooth-topped tanks without turrets, designed to move up against a high wall or other obstacle to provide a piggyback surface for following tanks to climb. Petards mounted huge mortars, while crocodiles carried outsized flame throwers; both were extremely useful against enemy pillboxes and strong points.

All the funnies put together made an impressive difference in winning a quick foothold on a defended beach. Without them it is quite possible that many sectors of the British beaches would have been as near-disastrous as Omaha.

Juno was a costly target for the 3rd Canadian Division. Once again, many of the DD tanks failed to survive the

The Gold Beach sector was still being raked by mortar and machine-gun fire when this picture was taken. Troops move grimly up the beach past the dead and wounded.

choppy seas. The underwater obstacles could not be cleared, but fortunately they were spaced widely enough so that landing craft could slip in between them. The first invasion waves were able to move up past the beach and on to Courseulles, where bitter house-to-house fighting held them up for several hours before they continued inland.

The Canadians tended to move more swiftly than the British regulars, but this was not a matter of courage or energy. As one observer said, "The British had been fighting Germans since 1940. Most of them were utterly fearless, but they were seldom in a hurry. They were used to war. They were glad they had finally landed in France, but they expected to be there for some time and they couldn't get overexcited about the immediacy of taking particular objectives."

This did not mean that the British soldier would not rise to the occasion.

In the water color at left a Sherman tank and a wrecker for recovering damaged vehicles roll inland from Gold Beach. The British invaders employed specialized tanks called "funnies." Two types are shown above: flail tanks (foreground and left) cleared mine fields; bridging tanks (background) spanned streams.

One of the exits from Juno was cut by a wide stream that was holding up the infantry. A tank misgauged the depth of the water and sank nearly out of sight. But this accident gave the funnies a base to work on.

A bridging tank dumped the end of its span on the turret of the sunken tank, and fascines filled up the rest of the stream bed with logs. In a little over an hour the gap was bridged, and light tanks and infantry were moving across to drive the Germans farther back. Today, in summer when the stream is shallow, the rusting British tank is still visible beneath the surface.

At the eastern end of Gold, a casemated German 88-millimeter gun, an exceptionally deadly antitank weapon, was picking off British tanks almost at will as they landed. Captain Roger Bell, in a flail tank, saw what was happening and reacted more by impulse than by any standard military practice.

117

Bell drove to within one hundred yards of the emplacement and opened fire with his tank gun; at that range the 88 could have blown him off the beach, but the Germans ignored the strange-looking vehicle and concentrated on the regular tanks instead. The Captain fired two high-explosive rounds directly at the enemy position. They seemed to have no effect, and the 88 continued firing. Bell then switched to armor-piercing shells and slammed three rounds into the casemate. Before he could fire again, another British tank lumbered across his sights. As he watched breathlessly, it went on its way, unharmed. The 88 had been silenced, and Bell rolled on to help clear mine fields.

Sword had a full complement of German defensive positions, but here the DD tanks—twenty-eight out of forty-four landed successfully—were able to knock out most enemy positions in the first fifteen minutes after landing. Here, too, the Luftwaffe put on its biggest show of D-Day. Two hours after the first landings, eight Junkers 88 attack bombers zoomed over the beach dropping bombs. Casualties were slight, however, and the raid was not repeated.

British landings farther east continued the successful invasion pattern.

Field Marshal Rommel reacted strongly to the British drive on Caen. Below, German self-propelled artillery—assault guns mounted on tank chassis—moves into Normandy. At right, an ammunition truck accompanying a British armored column explodes after taking a direct hit from an enemy mortar.

SPEIDEL, *Invasion: 1944*

Seaborne troops linked up with Colonel Otway's paratroopers, who had silenced the Merville battery on the far side of the Orne delta, and dug in securely along the east bank of the river. Commando units put the other bank of the river under British control. Strong German emplacements in the once carefree resort village of Riva Bella were subdued by DD and flail tanks doing a job that would have taken unsupported infantry troops hours or even days.

A spectacular reunion took place at the Caen Canal bridge, which had been held by the airborne invaders for nearly twelve hours. Lord Simon Lovat, whose commandos were piped onto the beach by their own bagpipers, had promised to relieve the troops at the canal bridge by noon, and Lord Lovat was a Scotsman who believed in keeping his word.

He marched his men out of the Sword Beach sector as soon as their work there was wound up, and with the pipes screeching "Blue Bonnets over the Border," headed for his rendezvous. The canal bridge was four miles away, but Lovat's force moved blithely through and around pockets of German resistance as though it were on a Highland outing.

German counterattacks were giving

While the beaches were being secured, patrols probed inland. Above, British commandos advance under sniper fire to clear a village. The most hazardous assignments were given these specially trained troops.

St. Aubin (upper right), a resort between Juno and Sword beaches, lay in ruins by the time infantrymen moved in to flush out the last German resistance. Its streets were blocked by log antitank barriers.

British patrols used bicycles to speed their advance once they reached the roads inland. In the photograph at right, a scouting party moves off the beach past a battered farmhouse and a wrecked troop carrier.

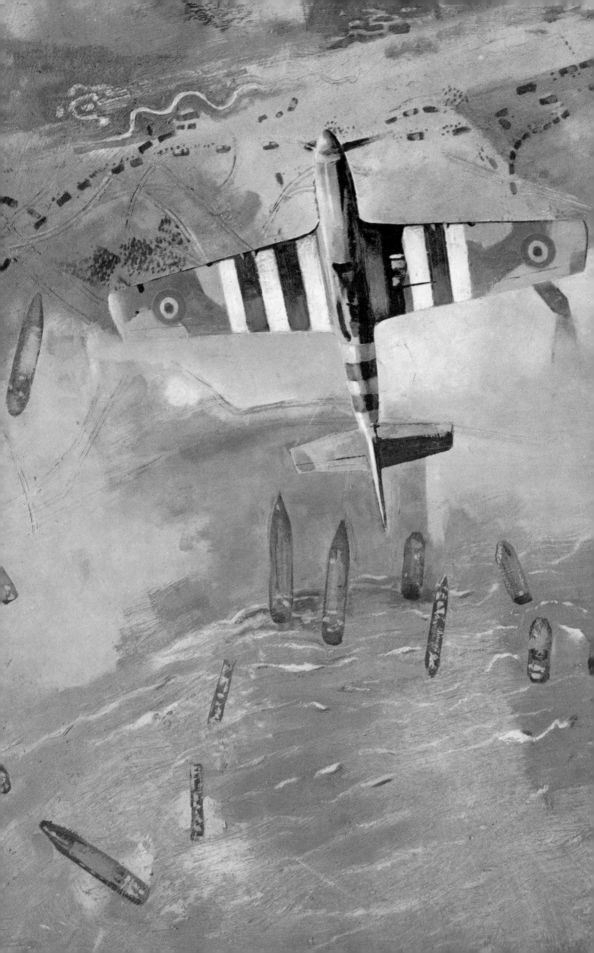

the paratroops and glider men at the bridge a highly uncomfortable morning. At 1:30 in the afternoon a bewildered paratrooper claimed he heard a bagpipe. It was only moments later when the whole bridge guard knew they they heard a bagpipe. "Blue Bonnets over the Border" skirled through the French air, and down the road from the sea strode Lord Lovat. A great cheer went up, and the Germans were so thunderstruck by the sight that they stopped shooting.

Their guns were quickly back at work, but by that time Lovat's commandos had joined the bridge guard. Lovat apologized courteously for being late for his appointment. There was still hard fighting ahead for both units — the rest of the invading forces would not catch up until late afternoon— but the link-up put new heart into the airborne troops after their weary and confusing night.

The Germans made their one major D-Day counterattack in the afternoon. The British sector seemed to pose the most immediate threat, and it was against it that the Germans launched the 21st Panzer Division. This armored group had served with Rommel in the North African campaign and now stood to the southeast of Caen under orders to counterattack any invasion.

Rommel himself was speeding as fast as he could to his Normandy headquarters. He stopped en route at Rheims to telephone for news from the beaches. When he came out after the call, it was clear that the news had been bad. Resuming the drive, he said to his aide, "If the 21st Panzer can make it, we might just be able to drive them back in three days."

It was the voice of forlorn hope, and in any case, the 21st Panzer did not make it. It might have, for when it first prepared to counterattack there was a vulnerable gap between Juno and Sword. But a mix-up in orders delayed the take-off of the 21st, and it lost still more time by having to bypass Caen, already in rubble from Allied air raids.

A few German tanks managed to get all the way to the beach, but the thrust had lost too much time and had allowed the British to get set. Antitank fire stopped the main column in its tracks, knocked out ten tanks, and forced the Germans to withdraw. As they dug in for the night, the Panzer troops saw silvery swarms of British gliders swooping down in the fading light to safe landing fields between the Germans and the sea.

Captured German prisoners worked

A U.S.-built Mustang fighter, marked with invasion stripes and British insignia, sweeps across the Normandy shore. On the beach below are truck convoys and emptied landing craft waiting to be refloated by the high tide.

NATIONAL GALLERY OF CANADA

OVERLEAF: *Tracers crisscross the night sky over a British-held village in the Sword sector as antiaircraft gunners go to work on attacking German planes. The Luftwaffe was too weakened to mount major daylight raids.*

IMPERIAL WAR MUSEUM

in the surf under the direction of British engineers, removing the beach obstacles that they and their comrades had planted weeks and months before to repel an invasion. Some of the Germans would be moved across to England that night, the first lap of a journey to a prisoner-of-war camp in the United States or Canada.

Rommel reached his headquarters at La Roche-Guyon in time to hear the last bad news. It had been a long day, and now it was evening—evening for Hitler's Third Reich and for Field Marshal Rommel's career.

The British had missed some of their objectives, but they had done a highly professional job of winning, holding, and enlarging the twenty-mile stretch of beach. The areas under their control ran from five to six miles inland, and individual units and armored patrols had penetrated half again as far. The Canadians were parked virtually on the doorstep of Caen. The British 50th Division had just barely missed taking Bayeux, so close a miss that one more day would see it accomplished.

England's terrible memory of defeat in France in 1940, the scar of Dieppe, the long, hard years of waiting—all had been made up for in this day's action. What was evening for Rommel and the Germans was the beginning of a new day for the Allies.

French citizens watch a column of Sherman tanks of the British 2nd Army, massed for the assault on Caen, rumbling through the narrow streets of their village on June 8.

127

Their beachhead secure, the Allies poured reinforcements ashore by the thousands. Aaron Bohrod painted this antlike column of newly landed American infantrymen, led by an ambulance, crawling up a battle-scarred hill behind Omaha.

7.

Road to Victory

The sixth of June was a day to carve into history, a day that marked a change in the tide of men and nations to stand for all time alongside such battles as Marathon and Hastings and Waterloo in the annals of the western world.

There could be no more talk of Fortress Europe; the fortress had been breached, and the invaders were being reinforced almost without interference. D-Day was a long step on the road to victory over Adolf Hitler's mad dream of ruling the world. Never before in the history of warfare had there been an operation like this one in scope, in complexity, and now in success.

Less than fifty years before, a New York newspaper had written with glowing pride of the campaign in Cuba during the Spanish-American War: "General Shafter and his officers have accomplished almost a miracle in landing sixteen thousand soldiers with food, arms, ammunition and equipment in small boats through a rough surf on the steep dangerous beach, between ugly reefs in almost killing heat. . . . The work was all done and well done in four days."

In Normandy, by the end of D-Day, the Allies had landed roughly 200,000 men on beaches not merely steep and dangerous, but defended by enemy troops and dominated by massive gun emplacements. Behind the beaches, about 33,000 airborne troops, dropped by parachute or soaring in by glider, were sowing confusion in the enemy camp and fighting to link up fully with the beach forces. The total Allied strength landed in one day was greater than the force the Germans thought could be moved across the Channel in a week.

Utah Beach was an organized military base. Most of its original combat troops had moved on, combining with paratroopers to repel German counter-thrusts and advancing north and west and south. Signalmen, engineers, medical detachments, and quartermaster units were turning the newly won stretch of sand into a landing port for the fresh waves of combat troops and fighting vehicles pouring ashore.

The beachhead at Omaha was longer and less deep, but it was tough despite its thinness. Along the shore line there were still dangerous pockets of resistance, German gun positions shaken but not knocked out by the bombardments and assaults of the previous day. But now the Yanks had the confidence of possession as well as tanks, artillery, and infantry to clean up the remaining shore defenses. They fought through to join British troops in taking Bayeux on June 7.

Although the British had failed to take Caen, their repulse of the 21st Panzer Division counterattack at

Sword, and their considerable success on all three of their beaches, was highly satisfactory. It was clear from the withdrawal of the Panzers that the German Army was now on the defensive. It must fight to hold on to what it had before it could think of throwing the invaders back into the sea according to von Rundstedt's unrealistic dream.

Survey work was already under way off Omaha and the British beaches, preparing for the arrival and assembly of the huge concrete artificial harbors, or Mulberries. Gooseberries, the breakwaters and temporary moorings formed by sinking ancient ships offshore, were begun for all three of the landing areas.

Field Marshal Rommel was back at his headquarters, trying to bring some kind of order to the defense. Even now the German command could not rid itself of the belief that troops must be held east of Normandy to protect the Calais area. Rommel did analyze Caen as a major threat, and he focused enough German power there to hold off the British for weeks from an objective that quite possibly might have fallen with an extra push on D-Day.

But neither this nor other German countermeasures could stem an invasion that built up an irresistible drive from the base of its first victories. In less than two weeks the Allies poured ashore over 625,000 men, 95,000 vehicles of all kinds, and 218,000 tons of supplies. Their strength in the air remained overwhelming, and the big guns of the battleships stationed

One of the huge concrete sections of Mulberry A, the artificial harbor at Omaha Beach, is towed into place on June 19. Almost immediately, a three-day hurricane struck and demolished the half-completed Mulberry. A second harbor located off the British beaches was damaged but survived the storm.

GIs broke into Carentan (left) on June 12, the same day that Allied war leaders visited the beachhead. Above, from left, are U.S. Air Force chief "Hap" Arnold, Navy head Ernest King, General Eisenhower, and Army chief of staff George Marshall. Below is England's Winston Churchill.

A week after D-Day the British 2nd Army thrust forward to flank the enemy forces defending Caen. In this water color a patrol, guarded by a Sherman tank (background), pushes through a village. The German tank at left is the greatly feared Panther type, abandoned after losing a tread to antitank fire.

offshore continued to be trump cards.

The Allies soon had over fourteen divisions in Normandy, and the Germans only thirteen; and the Allies were able to move reinforcements across the Channel more quickly than the Germans could bring in men and guns and vehicles over the roads and railways gutted by Allied air raids.

German submarines hurried into the Channel to break up the continuous traffic from English ports to Normandy, but Allied air and sea defenses made short shrift of their mission. Six U-boats were sunk from the air and six more severely damaged. More ships were lost to weather and accidental collision than from German attacks in the Channel. The Allies had won the battle of the beaches; now they were winning the equally important battle of supply.

How and why had Overlord succeeded against a tough enemy who had had four years to prepare for such an invasion, and who had within striking distance a superiority in men and equipment? While the over-all analysis is nearly as complicated and weighty as the reams of paper that went into D-Day planning, certain reasons stand out clearly.

For one thing, the Normandy assault came as a total surprise to the defenders. The Pas-de-Calais bluff had worked. Not only the place but the timing of the attack was successful. General Eisenhower's gamble to go ahead in spite of the threatening weather had paid off, for June 6 had been written off by the German high command as an impossible invasion date.

A seaborne invasion is as difficult an operation as anything in modern warfare, and taken as a whole, the planning of the Normandy assault was an incredible feat. Nothing on such a scale had ever been attempted before. Today it is hard to believe or even imagine that great armada of some 5,000 vessels of every shape and size and description crossing almost one hundred miles of storm-churned water without being detected.

Another Allied advantage was the rigidity of German thinking—not simply the fatal fixation on the Pas-de-Calais, but the disciplined rigidity all down the line which failed over and over again when faced with the unexpected.

Many of the Allied air drops might have been wiped out before they became a threat had the defenders attempted independent action. But they did not; while German command posts called headquarters to find out what they were to do, British and American airborne troops were given the time to pull together and then could not be dislodged.

The majority of the German soldiers manning the Atlantic Wall had fought hard and with courage, but they were badly served by the Nazi high command and particularly by Adolf Hitler. Both Rommel and von Rundstedt had pleaded for more men and equipment and for more flexible tactics. But Hitler could listen to no voice but his own.

TIME-LIFE COLLECTION, DEFENSE DEPAR'

War artist Aaron Bohrod painted Omaha as it looked on June 13, the hard-won beach now an efficient landing port. The German sign in the foreground warns of mines.

138

His fumbling kept the two armored divisions anchored far behind the lines until it was too late.

Another factor was the preinvasion bombardment by warships and planes on D-Day morning. This did damage enough to hamper an army far more imaginative than Hitler's. It was almost impossible to bring anything— men or equipment— into the invasion area by rail. German officers complained that roving fighter-bombers pounced on everything that moved by road, from tank columns to motorcycles.

The greatest single Allied tactical advantage, however, was the absence of the German Air Force. This was a matter of planned success, not of good luck. The British and American air forces based in England had achieved a superiority they were never to lose. Raids deep into Germany and her satellites hit the factories that made planes, destroyed planes on the ground and in the air, and blew up vital fuel supplies.

What remained of the once invincible Luftwaffe was a fragment that portly Reichsmarshal Hermann Goer-

ing feared to risk. Even had he gambled on D-Day by hurling his available bombers and fighters against the beaches, it is doubtful that they could have evaded the protective cordon of Spitfires and Thunderbolts.

The final factor, one that can never be accurately gauged in advance or adequately honored afterward, was the bravery of the men who made the victory. The best plans, the finest equipment, the most favorable conditions, are only as good as the men who have to do the fighting.

There were medals aplenty earned all up and down the coast from Les Dunes de Varreville to Merville, but for every medal there were scores of men whose heroism went unsung and unnoticed in the smoke and dust and blood-stained waters on D-Day.

One naval officer, in his reaction to the landing at Omaha, probably speaks for thousands of Allied invaders. "After I had one good look at the smoke and the flashes from the guns and the bodies drifting in the surf," he said, "I was quite sure I was going to

An American antitank gun blasts a German position during the drive into the Cotentin Peninsula to capture the port of Cherbourg. Rommel had radioed the defenders, "You will continue to fight until the last cartridge"; as a result the battle was a savage and bloody one.

U.S. ARMY

OVERLEAF: *In late July the U.S. 1st Army finally broke out of the Normandy beachhead. Sherman tanks are shown here pushing through shattered St. Lô as German prisoners (right) are herded to the rear. In the left background is the shell of the city's historic cathedral.*

TIME-LIFE COLLECTION, DEFENSE DEPARTMENT

die right there. As soon as I knew this, I felt fairly free and capable, so I got to work doing everything I could."

This brand of bravery was probably most obvious at Omaha, where each new wave refused to believe in the seemingly hopeless odds; but it raised its banner everywhere that day, from the beaches to the marshlands and the hedgerows far inland. Courage and ingenuity, more than anything else, won the Allies their foothold on Normandy.

Yet, for all its bravery and amazing achievement, a foothold was all it was. There remained all of France, Germany itself, and German holdings all over Europe still to be tackled and won. The job of the first days was threefold. First, to link up the landing beaches, organize them, and bring them up to their full potential as temporary ports; second, to hold off enemy counterattacks; and third, to continue the movement inland. The immediate objectives of the movement inland were to secure Caen and the area around it and to capture the important port of Cherbourg at the tip of the Cotentin Peninsula.

German concentration for the defense of Caen was heavy. It prevented the British from taking this target for over a month, but the German manpower it absorbed made the American offensive against Cherbourg easier.

Here the aim was to sever the peninsula, by taking and holding a line due west from Utah, and then to drive into the confined area and take Cherbourg. The Germans could have interfered with this plan by throwing in the two Panzer divisions, but the high command held the Panzers near Caen, hypnotized by two fears— of General Montgomery, who had chased them out of North Africa, and of a second invasion strike in the Pas-de-Calais.

Rommel and von Rundstedt both wanted to pull back and consolidate their troops to gain time to organize a knockout blow against the Allies, but they were overruled by Hitler. As he had done before with disastrous results on other war fronts, the Fuehrer refused to let his troops yield an inch of territory, no matter what the strategic value of such a withdrawal.

By June 8 the Allies were ready to punch toward Carentan from east and north in an all-out effort to link the beachheads together. This action took five days of bitter fighting in which the Allies used warships, tanks, artillery, planes— and the ever-present infantrymen. Carentan fell on June 12, and the

Reminders of the desperate struggle of the sixth of June were visible long after the Allied armies had advanced inland. In the painting at top, French civilians visit a shell-torn World War I military cemetery overlooking Omaha Beach. At right, wrecked assault craft lying beneath Omaha's cliffs give the beach itself the look of a graveyard.

Ogden Pleissner sketched the Nazi tank above, and its dead crew, at St. Lô. The three-stage Normandy breakout is pictured on the map at right. Phase one: the U.S. 1st Army seizes the Cotentin Peninsula, Cherbourg, and St. Lô. Phase two: American forces drive into Brittany and to Le Mans; then, in conjunction with the British advancing from Caen, they mangle the German 7th Army in the "Falaise Pocket." Phase three: the Allied armies sweep eastward and, by the end of August, take Paris and cross the Seine above and below the French capital.

Allies now gripped a full seventy miles of sea front with a depth varying from five to ten miles.

The capture of this objective was the start of the next, the cutting off of the peninsula. It was an infantry struggle every step of the way. The terrain to be taken was the deadly Normandy pattern of marsh and hedgerow and small villages. Tanks and artillery and air support gave vital assistance, but in this kind of country, it was the foot soldier who had to take each enemy position and make it secure before going on to the next.

From Carentan, Americans slashed across the base of the peninsula toward the coast, while other units held down German divisions in a savage struggle for St. Lô; still other troops turned right and made for Cherbourg.

It took another major naval bombardment before Cherbourg finally fell on June 26. The Allies had the first major port they needed. Early in July, the British 2nd Army succeeded in

THE BREAKTHROUGH

N

ENGLAND

London

ENGLISH

CHANNEL

Dunkirk

Calais

Boulange

PAS-DE-CALAIS

Somme R.

Cherbourg

Le Havre

Rouen

Carentan

Bayeux

Dives R.

Seine R.

Caen

St. Lô

NORMANDY

Orne R.

Vire R.

Falaise

Paris

St. Malo

Avranches

Eure R.

Chartres

Rennes

'TANY

Le Mans

Orléans

Loir R.

F R A N C E

Nantes

Loire R.

0   10   20   30   40   50

MILES

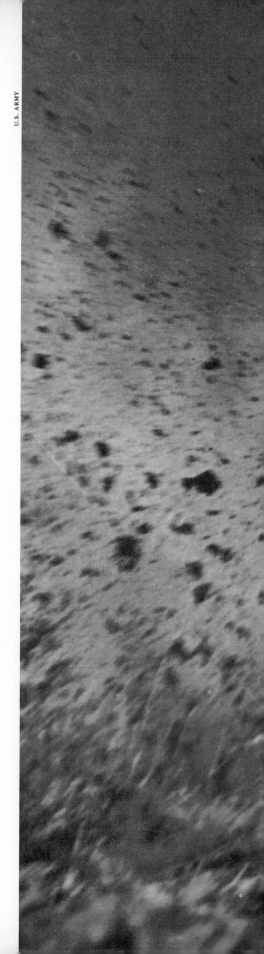

its assault on Caen; by July 18, St. Lô had fallen to the American 1st Army.

The taking of St. Lô broke one end of the German defense line and set the stage for the Allied breakthrough into central France. The biggest goals still lay ahead — Paris, the Rhine, and the industrial heart of Germany — but the whole tone of the war had changed.

Utah and Omaha, Gold, Juno, and Sword were on the way to becoming glorious names for the history books; their duties as landing beaches were almost over by late autumn. Engineers were busy repairing the damage the Germans had left behind in Cherbourg and in newly taken Le Havre, getting them in shape to unload the stream of transports already putting in.

Omaha closed down as a landing port on November 22. Utah had already been allowed slowly to go out of business. The British Mulberry soon joined them.

Fresh troops coming into Le Havre or Cherbourg in November could hardly imagine what it had been like six months before on the beaches between the two efficient ports. The Third Reich had but six months more to live, a fact made possible by the dogged courage of the invading soldiers in those uncertain and terrible hours of early morning on the sixth of June.

While there was bitter fighting ahead for the Allies in Europe, D-Day marked the beginning of the end for Nazi Germany. In this photograph, taken in Holland, an American GI advances under a hail of enemy shells.

146

British soldiers direct artillery fire against enemy positions in Normandy.

AMERICAN HERITAGE PUBLISHING·CO., INC.

BOOK DIVISION

Editor

Richard M. Ketchum

———— * ————

JUNIOR LIBRARY

Editor

Stephen W. Sears

Art Director

Emma Landau

Assistant Editors John Ratti · Mary Lee Settle

Picture Researchers Julia B. Potts, *Chief*
Dennis A. Dinan · Mary Leverty

Copy Editor Patricia Cooper

ACKNOWLEDGMENTS

The Editors are especially indebted to the following individuals and organizations for their generous assistance and advice in preparing this book:

Colonel Vincent J. Esposito, Department of Military Art and Engineering, U. S. Military Academy, West Point.

Mrs. Maureen Green, London

Department of the Air Force, Washington — Major Gene Guerny, Mrs. Grace Brenner

Department of the Army, Washington — Colonel R.H. Wiltamuth, Lt. Colonel Hubert J. Van Kan, Mrs. Marian McNaughton, Mrs. Donna Traxler

Department of the Navy, Washington — Lt. Commander F.A. Prehn, Charles Lawrence

United States Coast Guard, Washington — Commander J.D. Doyle, Elizabeth Segedi

Library of Congress, Washington — Virginia Daiker

National Archives (U.S. Navy files), Washington — Walter Barbasch

National Archives (World War II Records Division), Alexandria, Va. — Sherrod East, Richard Bauer

Royal Canadian Air Force, Ottawa — R.V. Dodds

Royal Canadian Army, Ottawa — Lt. Colonel F.K. Reesor, Captain William Wright

Royal Canadian Navy, Ottawa — R. Stead

National Gallery of Canada, Ottawa — R.H. Hubbard, R.F. Wodehouse

Imperial War Museum, London — A.J. Charge, J.F. Golding, W.P. Mayes

National Maritime Museum (Department of Prints), Greenwich, England

FOR FURTHER READING

This list is divided into two categories. The first part includes the more readable accounts of the D-Day invasion, plus general World War II books which shed light on the events of the sixth of June and on the people involved in that great battle. The second category is a selection of official military histories. As important as these histories are to a complete understanding of Operation Overlord, they tend to be — with the notable exception of Admiral Morison's work — highly technical.

Bradley, Omar N. *A Soldier's Story.* Henry Holt, 1951.

Colby, Carroll Burleigh. *Fighting Gear of World War II.* Coward-McCann, 1961.

Churchill, Winston S., and the editors of *Life. The Second World War* (Vol. II). Time Inc., 1959.

Eisenhower, Dwight D. *Crusade in Europe.* Doubleday, 1948.

Esposito, Vincent J., editor. *The West Point Atlas of American Wars* (Vol. II). Praeger, 1959.

Hart, B.H. Liddell, editor. *The Rommel Papers.* Harcourt, Brace, 1953.

Howarth, David. *D Day, The Sixth of June.* McGraw-Hill, 1959.

Kirk, John, and Young, Robert, editors. *Great Weapons of World War II.* Walker, 1961.

Marshall, S.L.A. *Night Drop.* Atlantic-Little, Brown, 1962.

Norman, Albert. *Operation Overlord.* Military Service Publishing Company, 1952.

Pawle, Gerald. *The Secret War.* William Sloane, 1957.

Ryan, Cornelius. *The Longest Day.* Simon and Schuster, 1959.

Speidel, Hans. *Invasion 1944.* Henry Regnery, 1950.

Sterling, Dorothy, editor. *I Have Seen War: 25 Stories from World War II.* Hill and Wang, 1960.

Tregaskis, Richard. *Invasion Diary.* Random House, 1944.

Wertenbaker, Charles Christian. *Invasion!* Appleton-Century-Crofts, 1944.

☆　☆　☆　☆　☆　☆　☆

Craven, Wesley F., and Cate, James L., editors. *The Army Air Forces in World War II* (Vol. III). University of Chicago Press, 1951.

Harrison, Gordon A. *Cross-Channel Attack. (The United States Army in World War II).* Department of the Army, 1951.

Morison, Samuel Eliot. *The Invasion of France and Germany.* (Vol. XI of *History of United States Naval Operations in World War II*). Atlantic-Little, Brown, 1957.

Roskill, S.W. *The War at Sea.* (Vol. III, Part II, United Kingdom Military Series). Her Majesty's Stationery Office, 1961.

A portrait of the real hero of D-Day— the lowly infantryman.

101ST AIRBORNE DIVISION

Index

Bold face indicates pages on which illustrations appear

Axis powers, 11, 12

B

Barrage balloons, 14, **76-77**
Bayeux, France, 107, 127, 130
Bayfield, 71
Beach obstacles, **front endsheet, 18, 20,** 70,
   79, 80, 88, 89, **89, 90-91,** 99, 109, 116, 127
"Beetles," 70, **71**
Bell, Capt. Roger, 117-118
Black Prince, 39, 43, 65
Bradley, Lt. Gen. Omar, **15,** 71, 92, 93, **94**
Brest, France, 16, 35
British Beaches, 45, 48-49 (map), 52, 53, 106-
   107 (map), 109, 116, 118, 123, 127, 142
British troops
   2nd Army, 134, 144
   3rd Division, 105
   50th Division, 105, 107
   3rd Canadian Division, 105, 114
   6th Airborne Division, 46, 49, 50, 60
   Commandos, 105, 109, **110,** 119, **120,** 123
   See also Paratroopers, Royal Navy
Bulldozers, 88, 89, 99
Buoy Ships, 37, 78

C

Caen, France, 46, 99, 107, 123, 127, 130,
   142, 144
Caen Canal bridge, 46, 49, 51, **51,** 119, 123
Calais, France, 16
Camin, Pvt. John, 60
Campbell, 37
Canadian troops, **107,** 116, 127. *See also* Brit-
   ish troops
Canham, Col. Charles, 95
Capa, Robert, 83, 91
Carentan, France, 53, 63, **132-133,** 142, 144
Cherbourg, France, 25, 139, 142, 144, 146
Churchill, Prime Minister Winston, 34, **133**
Collins, Maj. Gen. J. Lawton, 71
Commandos, *see* British troops
Communications, Allied, 52, 71, 83, 88, 92,
   93
Communications, German, 68, 74
Corry, 39, 43
Cota, Brig. Gen. Norman, 95, 99
Cotentin Peninsula, 30, 46, 139, 142
Courseulles, France, 116

D

DD tank, *see* "Funnies"
D-Day, 25, 26. *See also* Neptune, Normandy
   Invasion
DeGaulle, Gen. Charles, 14
Deyo, Rear Adm. Morton L., 43, 65
Dieppe, France, 111, 127
Dives River, 46, 49, 50, 52
Douve River, 59, 60
Dover, England, 19, 27, 30

E

Eisenhower, Gen. Dwight D., **7,** 12, 14, **15,**
   19, 23, 25, 45-46, **133,** 135
Emmons, **96-97**
Engineers, *see* U.S. Armed Forces
English Channel, 11, 19, 30, 35, 36, 50, 65
   Channel tides, 23, 34, 35, 73, 88, 109
   See also "Invasion Funnel," Neptune
Erebus, 65, 70
Etienville, France, 60

F

"Falaise Pocket," 144
Fitch, 39
Flame throwers, 18, 114
Fort St. Marcouf Battery, 26, 70
"Fortress Europe," 19, 27, 43, 71, 129
Foucarville, France, 58
Free French, 14, 19, 46, 78, 105, 109
French Resistance, 46
"Funnies," 111, 114, 117, **117,** 119
   DD tanks, **64-65,** 68, 80, 83, **90-91,** 111,
      114, 118, 119
   See also Tanks

G

Gavin, Brig. Gen. James A., 59
German Air Force, *see* Luftwaffe
German Army, 12, 59, 70
   Seventh Army, 26, 75, 77, 144
   Fifteenth Army, 26, 74
   21st Panzer Division, 123, 130, 142
   352nd Division, 87, 99, 101
   716th Division, 111
German High Command, 74, 130, 135
German Intelligence, 15, 71
German Navy, 39, 109
Gliders, 19, 49, **50, 51,** 53, **56-57, 58,** 60, **61**